GREAT MEN OF SCIENCE, NOS. 21 & 22

Glen Berger

BROADWAY PLAY PUBLISHING INC
New York
www.broadwayplaypublishing.com
info@broadwayplaypublishing.com

Cover image compliments of Circle X Theater, Los Angeles
First printing: April 2007
I S B N: 978-0-88145-291-4

Book design: Marie Donovan
Typeface: Palatino
Printed and bound in the U S A

The world premiere was originally produced by Circle X Theater in Los Angeles, opening on 19 March 1998. The cast and creative contributors were:

CHATELET . . . . Alice Dodd
VAUCANSON . . . . Matthew Allen Bretz
SPALLANZANI . . . . Jim Anzide
CONDORCET . . . . David Paul Wichert
LECAT . . . . .Paul Morgan Stetler
HOUSEKEEPER . . . . Melanie Van Betten
ABBE . . . . Bob Clendenin

Director . . . . .Jillian Armenante
Stage Manager . . . . Anne Mulhall
Set Designer . . . . .Gary Smoot
Costume Designer . . . . M E Dunn
Lighting Designer . . . . .Dan Weingarten
Sound Designers . . . . Daniel Hakim & Mikael Sandgren
Music Selection .Jillian Armenante

The production received a Theater L A Ovation Award for Best Production in a Small Theater and two L A Weekly Awards for Production of The Year and Playwriting.

Original poster design by Nichole Hagedorn

SUMMARY

Battling obstacles both grand and trivial in eighteenth century France, two little-known scientists strive mightily to advance humanity's understanding of life and the universe in GREAT MEN OF SCIENCE, NOS. 21 & 22. In 1738, at the heady height of the Age of Enlightenment, the Royal Academy of Sciences has announced its annual contest—to prove or refute that behind the seeming randomness of all creation, there is God's wisdom and design. JACQUES DE VAUCANSON attempts to prove the assertion, and thereby win the love of the woman he adores, by constructing the first biologically accurate automata—a clockwork duck that flaps its wings, eats, and excretes just like a duck. Years later, during the blackest months of the Reign of Terror, a bitter and elderly LAZARRO SPALLANZANI studies mating frogs to understand once and for all how life is conceived, and discovers instead the significance his longtime housekeeper has played in his life.

A minimum of six actors is required.

ACT ONE

Life, the Canard

The Story of Jacques de Vaucanson's Great Labour

CHARACTERS & SETTING

Jacques de Vaucanson
Gabrielle du Chatelet
Abbe
Le Cat
Lazarro Spallanzani
Citizens #1-#4, Member of Academy, etc.

Note for ACT ONE *set: Slide projection suggested. Consider as well utilizing projection screen as a screen for eighteenth century-style silhouette-tableaus.*

Note for ACT ONE *music: Music is strongly recommended for the production. Modern, yet evoking the eighteenth-century, intricate, repetitive, and stirring.*

Time: 1738

(Lights up slowly to reveal GABRIELLE DU CHATELET, *dressed as the Goddess of Reason. She sings—)*

CHATELET: *(Singing)* Awake my Paris...
Stir from thy slumberings!
The worlds you now strive in
Shall be snuffed and forgotten
come the Dawn....
Bid farewell and return to
This one Dream we share...
Paris....Awake....

Embrace the streets
Embrace the anvils
And sewers
And markets
And furnaces

(Light up on VAUCANSON *asleep in thinking pose)*

CHATELET: And you...Jacques de Vaucanson...
Great hope of our time...
Whose mind burns with the
Incandescency
Of Genius...
Now Dispel the mists from your eyes
So you may dispel the great mist from ours
So we may be brought
Ever nearer...ever nearer...
To the Age of Light...
Leave your dreams behind....
Behold! ...The world...is thine....

(We see drawings of Moon and Sun. A ticking watch increases anticipation:)

VAUCANSON: With its face always facing us, The Moon in this Minuet, moving counterclockwise, six tenths of a mile with every tick of the clock, bids Paris *adieu* for the day, and now we bow to the Sun, and Morning comes as Morning must!

(The city awakes with cock crow and stirring music. VAUCANSON conjectures to himself in his studio, perhaps utilizing quill and paper—)

VAUCANSON: *(Conjecturing, not narrating)* A hammer, in a thirty-four degree arc, strikes a nail, one two three four times and Pause....

(We see a man hammering a notice of heavy paper, one two three four times, pause. Then silence while—)

VAUCANSON: ...And in the pause, in a puddle...the birth of a gnat. For now, at least, it lives. A fifth time hammer to nail and one more for good measure—

(The hammerer hammers once and one more for good measure)

HAMMERER: The Annual Contest, sponsored by the Royal Academy of Sciences, has today been made public! Devised for the year of our Lord Seventeen Hundred Thirty Eight!

CITIZEN #1: *(Reading notice)* "With the highest Degree of Persuasiveness, Prove or Refute the following statement, uttered by the eminent mathematician Abraham de Moivre—"

(Projected on a screen, or on a large banner unfurled, De Moivre's statement is written, and visible throughout the play. We hear the voice of De Moivre, and, perhaps, see a rendering of De Moivre, with moving mouth)

VOICE OF DE MOIVRE: "The Apparent *Randomness* of Events in Nature—

CITIZENS: The Apparent Randomness—

VOICE OF DE MOIVRE: Will, if subjected to Calculation, Reveal an *underlying Order* Expressing Exquisite Wisdom and Design."

CITIZEN #1: *(Reading)* "Prove or Refute."

(For the following section, CITIZENS #1-#5 move with precision in a sort of minuet in the "street". ABBE is to the side, unseen by citizens. VAUCANSON remains in studio.)

CITIZEN #2: What minds have turned to this question!

CITIZEN #3: To prove or refute is to prove or refute the existence of God—

VAUCANSON: Dear Lord grant me the courage and wherewithal to unveil Your secrets.... Surely You do not mean them to be secrets forever.... And surely now our gnat touches down on a hat. The right elbow bends, the hand is carried upward, and by pressure of thumb, the hat, with the gnat...is lifted.

(The right elbow of ABBE bends, he takes off hat and bows)

CITIZEN #4: *(To CITIZEN #2)* Have you heard from D'Alembert?

CITIZEN #2: *(Excitedly)* Oh yes—in affirmation of DeMoivre, he will show that Newton's Third Law of Motion applies to both freely-moving *and* stationary bodies.

CITIZEN #1: And what, pray tell, of Fontanelle—

CITIZEN #3: —the secretary of the Royal Academy is refuting the possibility that random events are anything but random. He said, and I quote, "It is beyond the reach of scientific investigation.

VAUCANSON: A gnat in the nose and a sneeze!

*(*ABBE *sneezes)*

CITIZEN #1: And what of Jacques de Vaucanson?

VAUCANSON: A sneeze.

*(*ABBE *sneezes)*

CITIZEN #1: And what of Jacques de Vaucanson?

(Long pause)

VAUCANSON: A sneeze.

(And an enormous sneeze from ABBE*)*

CITIZEN #4: Jacques de Vaucanson!

CITIZEN #2: A most promising young scientist—

CITIZEN #4: Startling—

CITIZEN #3: Insolent—

CITIZEN #1: Jacques de Vaucanson!

CITIZEN #2: Yet I have heard he has over-reached himself this time—

CITIZEN #3: It is a mathematical problem, and he is known for mechanical things—

CITIZEN #1: His rooms have been given over to every manner of machinery—

CITIZEN #3: He returns his meals uneaten—

CITIZEN #1: Only the Jesuit, the Abbe deFontaine, knows just what he labours on—

CITIZEN #4: Yes, the Abbe, whose fondness for Vaucanson is rivaled only by his fondness for a drink—

(The ABBE, *a dissipated older Jesuit, enters, carrying a parcel under his arm and putting a flask surreptitiously to his lips)*

CITIZEN #2: And I say! Isn't that the abbe now—

VAUCANSON: A gnat near the mouth now flies to the eye—

ABBE: I have been— *(He swats gnat by eye with hand)*

VAUCANSON: A miss.

ABBE: —requested by Monsieur Vaucanson not to reveal the nature of his work. You will see soon enough.

CITIZEN #3: And that parcel you conceal from us— is it not for your young upstart?

ABBE: You will see soon enough.

CITIZEN #1: But you must give us something!

ABBE: I gave him my word—

CITIZEN #2: But he's the only one missing from our list! *(He reads from his checklist, and checks "refute" or "affirm" in turn.)* Clairaut will examine the variables in magnesia and quicklime.

ALL: Refute!

CITIZEN #4: Maupertuis will address the case of the polygon curve.

ALL: Refute!

CITIZEN #4: Couboursier will account for the irregularities in the observed motion of the planets.

ALL: Affirm!

CITIZEN #4: Burke will forecast the month in 1751 when Halley's comet shall return—

ALL: Affirm!

CITIZEN #4: Lavoisier will show that Halley's comet shall never return—

ALL: A refutation!

VAUCANSON: If I can but do it—

CITIZEN #3: So you won't let on?

CITIZEN #2: Come come, what is Jacques concocting?

VAUCANSON: If I can but do it—

CITIZEN #4: All of Paris wants to know—

VAUCANSON: Eyes will weep in gratitude—

CITIZEN #1: Divulge this at least: Will Vaucanson affirm or refute DeMoivre's statement?

CITIZEN #2: Will he affirm or refute DeMoivre's statement?!

(The music builds. We hear the rumble of carts on cobbles, the tension builds, and as church bells ring out across the city—)

ABBE: Affirm! He will affirm! And with a ringing declaration that will bring tears to the faithful and turn all the treatises of the Fontanelles and Buffons into so much bumf!

VAUCANSON: From the noblest man to the humblest gnat. Life!

CITIZEN #3: *(To* ABBE*)* Your neck, Monsieur.

*(*ABBE *swats neck, smashing gnat.)*

VAUCANSON: and Death—

ABBE: *(Exiting)* Good day!

(Music intensifies, isolated light on VAUCANSON*)*

VAUCANSON: *(Passionate to tears and heroism)* —Nothing is random.... Nothing is random, and I will prove it.... Employing Newton's laws of attraction by which the tides behave and the planets are known to rotate; Using calculations plotting the movement of the stars themselves across the heavens; Utilizing a system of springs and weights, gearwheels, cogs and escapements of my own construction fashioned in ratios of proven mathematical laws and proportion...I will create...a

Duck...that flaps its wings, eats, and excretes...just like a duck!

(The music ends, the stage clears. We then hear a number of insistent knocks on the door of the garret of VAUCANSON. *We become aware of the quack of ducks.* VAUCANSON *is deeply engrossed in hard thought and pained study and intense labor.)*

ABBE: *(Unseen, through door)* Monsieur Vaucanson, it is I —

VAUCANSON: *(Quite in the middle of work)* It's open.

ABBE: It's not open.

(Pause. Then knock knock knock)

VAUCANSON: It is open.

ABBE: Jacques it's locked.

VAUCANSON: It isn't. You have to push.

ABBE: I am. I am pushing.

VAUCANSON: No, push...push.

ABBE: I'm pushing.

VAUCANSON: Hold the handle and push.

ABBE: For God's sake, it is locked.

VAUCANSON: It is not locked. I was occasioned to unlock it an hour ago.

(Pause. More knocking. Pause)

ABBE: Jacques. The door is locked.

VAUCANSON: I'm telling you it's open, stop knocking and push.

ABBE: Jacques, we do not have much time—

VAUCANSON: *(Half to self)* I know...I know...in less than nine months I'm to present to the Academy a deterministic, dynamic model that yet will elucidate irregular, unpredictable behavior.... How...how to accomplish all that needs doing when I haven't a *sou* to my name and I've lost my peruke...

(Pause)

ABBE: What? Your what? Jacques, I can't hear you.... Look, I have something here to show you if you would only— *(Tries door again)* ...I think it will be a great aid in the solicitation of funds.... Please, I beg of you open the—

(VAUCANSON *pulls on door, unfastens bolt, opens door)*

VAUCANSON: It was locked after all. My apologies. Everywhere I turn, unexpected Impediments.

ABBE: You look terrible.

VAUCANSON: The work... The work involved...

ABBE: There's food outside the door—

VAUCANSON: Leave it outside.

ABBE: *(Retrieving it)* You must try to eat a little.

VAUCANSON: I cannot.

ABBE: When was the last time you ate?

VAUCANSON: I don't remember. I can't even look at it.

ABBE: It is nourishment.

VAUCANSON: Put it out of sight.

ABBE: If you want it, it's over here.

VAUCANSON: Fine.

ABBE: Do you see? Over here.

VAUCANSON: Fine!

ABBE: Jacques, how are you proceeding...

VAUCANSON: *(Erupts)* What contrivance can I use to make this artificial duck take up the corn and suck it up quite to its stomach I don't know! I don't know! I don't know! *(Calming)* ....the obstacles seem... insurmountable...

ABBE: But can you do it?

VAUCANSON: There is this. If I do not manage it, another will, in time. For all knowledge will be Man's, in time. I know I am at least fifty years ahead of my time. Perhaps sixty. But perhaps this idea of mine is eighty years ahead of its time.

ABBE: And what then?

VAUCANSON: I'll have no choice but endeavor to stride yet another twenty years in nine months and only hope it wasn't thirty years I needed to traverse.

ABBE: What? Look, Jacques, sleep, there's such a thing as that—

VAUCANSON: I know, but when I finish. If I finish.

ABBE: And then it will be the sleep of the just.

VAUCANSON: Oh more than that my friend, more than that. With such exuberance will the angels dance in Heaven that the crowns will fall off of their heads!

ABBE: And yet you do not believe in heaven.

VAUCANSON: Not as such. Sit and I will explain to you the whole of my beliefs.

ABBE: Jacques de Vaucanson doubles over, clutches his abdomen, profanes the Lord and takes off his trousers.

(VAUCANSON *doubles over in great pain*)

VAUCANSON: Jesus...God...! *(He hastens to unbutton trousers, and hops about from foot to foot to stifle the intense pain and refrain from urinating)*

ABBE: What is it? Do you need the chamberpot?

VAUCANSON: Where's the chamberpot....

ABBE: Is it your bladder again.

VAUCANSON: The stones, oh the stones... *(He finds chamberpot and runs behind the silhouette screen)*

ABBE: I thought you were improving...

VAUCANSON: No, if anything the spasms are more frequent.

ABBE: Haven't you seen a doctor?

VAUCANSON: No time. Or money....

ABBE: The suffering you endure...and yet still you continue...

VAUCANSON: *(With trousers at ankles, appearing from behind screen)* We must....We must persevere.... it is all we can do...

(He runs back behind screen. In silhouette, we see and hear Vaucanson urinating.)

VAUCANSON: *(Whilst urinating)* But what is this you were saying at the door—something about something to help us solicit funds?

ABBE: Oh yes, I was thinking we needed some sort of device to—

VAUCANSON: *(Due to volume of urinating)* What? I can't hear you—

ABBE: *(Raising voice to compete with urinating)* I was saying how I thought it would be —

VAUCANSON: I'm telling you, I can't hear you—

ABBE: *(Raising voice still louder)* Well just that it occurred to me—

VAUCANSON: Damn it, can't you see I'm occupied!?
A moment is all I ask!

(VAUCANSON *yelps in pain, finishes urinating, and emerges
trouserless.*)

ABBE: How are you?

VAUCANSON: Miserable.

ABBE: But are you taking anything for it?

VAUCANSON: *(Pulling out a small flask)* Just this.

ABBE: What is it?

VAUCANSON: Turpentine.

ABBE: Does it work?

VAUCANSON: In theory, it should break down the
stones, the stones being either calcium oxide or calcium
phosphate or magnesium ammonium phosphate but
I don't know. From time to time, I pass gravel. Perhaps
that is a good sign.

ABBE: Perhaps.

VAUCANSON: Well there's nothing to be done.

ABBE: Surgery?

VAUCANSON: Never again. But friend, what is this
about a device for raising money?

ABBE: I'm concerned about your gravel.

VAUCANSON: Never mind my gravel, if we can raise
enough money to enable the realization of this duck
I will be happy to pass the Alps in my urine. The Alps.

ABBE: Well. I thought to myself, how can we make our
plea for funds more compelling, and this old Jesuit
looked no further than another old Jesuit who
invented....this.

(*He opens the box he was carrying to reveal a Magic Lantern.*)

VAUCANSON: A Magic Lantern?

ABBE: What do you think?

(ABBE *has set up Magic Lantern and random slides are "projected"*)

VAUCANSON: I think in elucidating some of the finer points in our fund-raising presentations, yes the device of Jesuit mathematician, biologist and physicist Athanasius Kircher, who died in 1680, will be quite effective.

ABBE: *(Showing random slides)* And if not, the images can still be most pleasing to look upon. "If what we say is confusing to you, at least take solace in viewing this picture of... *(He changes the slide.)* ...a trout."

VAUCANSON: No! They must they must understand that we are furthering the case that God's world is not a whimsical and capricious one.

ABBE: And that of course is why, in the end, I am assisting you—

VAUCANSON: I do not deserve it. You have found suppliers and have been my invaluable liaison, you have raised much-needed funds, You have gone above and beyond—

ABBE: No, I'll hear no more of it. I once did you a terrible wrong.

(*A historical presentation utilizing magic lantern. We hear a hymn sung by a choir, and see slides depicting gears, orreries, angels, etc.:*)

ABBE: Jacques de Vaucanson, you once had designs of being a Jesuit. You were nine years old, a novice, and you constructed a mechanical angel. It opened its mouth in song and flapped its wings. "Just like an angel," you said. "Just like an angel indeed," said I. "How should you know how an angel flaps its wings?

How naive, how presumptuous, nay blasphemous,
to reduce a heavenly creature to cogs! Cogs and
gearwork!" "Look here you bitter ruinous old man,"
said you, "I wanted to see an angel come to life. You are
beholding a year's labour." "And now," said I, "you
will behold a moment's effort." And I smashed the
angel to pieces in front of you. And you, nine years old,
replied, "Father....Man and Woman once lived in a
Paradise. But this first paradise was *dependent* on their
ignorance. With the first taste of knowledge, they were
cast out. But it is you who are naive and presumptuous,
nay blasphemous, if you believe God constructed
this miracle of a world so that we may appreciate it
as a blind man appreciates a painting. Just as Newton
has revealed the laws governing the planets, that the
planets move with a clockwork precision, those same
laws must by necessity govern the natural world, and
when we at last fully understand these laws, we will
understand what God wants of us, what his intentions
are and what our purpose is, and when we understand
that, we will no longer be His helpless bawling child
groping in the darkness, but His *helpmate* and His true
friend and that will be the Second Paradise, the Lasting
Paradise, the paradise dependent not on ignorance, not
on ignorance, but on understanding, and we cannot
turn back, no, not out of fear, not now." And with that
you threw down your cassock, slammed the door, and
left the Jesuits, striding through the city streets to your
destiny.

VAUCANSON: Naked, for I wore nothing underneath my
cassock.

ABBE: Yes.

VAUCANSON: Impassioned.

ABBE: Yes.

VAUCANSON: And I have carried that vision to this day, and now this! —Something much better, something real and observable...something true...for yes like an angel, a duck too is God's creation, yes?

(Silence)

VAUCANSON: Why are you silent?

ABBE: I have just hit my funny bone. I am in great pain.

VAUCANSON: *(Out of patience with his friend)* Have you arranged a presentation.

ABBE: For next Tuesday, but I'll need a list from you tomorrow of the images we'll want to project, as well as a list of more necessary materials you require for your construction as another shipment goes out Friday.

VAUCANSON: Yes.

ABBE: And perhaps knowing there will be some money for your cogs and springs will permit you to sleep a bit easier?

VAUCANSON: Yes but... No...

ABBE: No?

VAUCANSON: No, for there is a further difficulty that threatens to undo all our good intentions....

ABBE: A further difficulty...

VAUCANSON: My ratios...I have lost all of my ratios.

ABBE: Your Ratios?

VAUCANSON: Yes...

ABBE: Are they important?

VAUCANSON: The duck cannot be made without them.

ABBE: And you cannot reconstitute the ratios?

VAUCANSON: Perhaps, but it would take me weeks of lost time, for they are built on discoveries that have taken me years to uncover through sweat and toil and miserable nights.

ABBE: And you don't know where you have misplaced them.

VAUCANSON: No...no, I know....

ABBE: You do know?

VAUCANSON: Yes.

ABBE: Then the difficulty—

VAUCANSON: The difficulty...the difficulty...oh god, the difficulty...is that...I am in love with Gabrielle-Emilie, the Marquise du Chatelet.

(Lights up on tableau of CHATELET*)*

VAUCANSON: She has green eyes and had Euclid and Virgil memorized before she was twelve.... Entrancing, enraging, and the first to translate Isaac Newton's Principia Mathematica into French...Who is like her? I...I never want to leave you.

*(*VAUCANSON *is now lying in bed. It is evening. Distant strains from a ball are heard. Perhaps a slide with title "Three Weeks Previous". The interaction between the two of them should feel as natural as possible.)*

CHATELET: But Jacques, your work—that must come first.

VAUCANSON: My work, yes. This contest of which you've just informed me intrigues. But how can I prove that events in nature are not random?

CHATELET: Not with pen and paper—

VAUCANSON: No, you're right, not a treatise..I need to create...a living testament!

CHATELET: Your submission to the Annual Contest will be nothing short of genius....

VAUCANSON: If I can but manage it.

CHATELET: You will.

VAUCANSON: I don't know.... Or no, yes, yes I will. I am with you and somehow nothing seems out of reach...Must we still keep the two of us a secret?

CHATELET: We must.

VAUCANSON: Your husband the Marquis.

CHATELET: My husband.

VAUCANSON: Come back to bed.

CHATELET: I am expected downstairs.

VAUCANSON: From here you can hear the ball—

CHATELET: But I'm the one who threw it—

VAUCANSON: You have set the dance in motion—now, as God does, let it run, in perfect harmony, without you.

CHATELET: *(Kissing him)* No...no...I really must return, and you must go—

VAUCANSON: I can't bear it!

CHATELET: Go forth and astonish the world.

VAUCANSON: I'll do my astonishing from this bed.

CHATELET: That's not what the Academy has in mind.

VAUCANSON: Who would even think to disprove DeMoivre?

CHATELET: Well, Fontanelle for one.

VAUCANSON: Let him try.

CHATELET: Francois Arouet for another...

VAUCANSON: Ah. Francois Arouet.

CHATELET: Yes. Francois Arouet.

VAUCANSON: Francois Arouet?

CHATELET: Yes, Francois Arouet.

(Pause)

VAUCANSON: By Francois Arouet you mean of course Voltaire.

CHATELET: Yes.

VAUCANSON: *(Feigning nonchalance)* So you have heard from him? Voltaire?

CHATELET: Yes.

VAUCANSON: So he is back from Prussia?

CHATELET: Yes.

VAUCANSON: And you have spoken with him.

CHATELET: I have spoken with him.

VAUCANSON: But did you not say yourself...
(Now erupting) that you were through with him?!

CHATELET: Only I can keep his imagination in check. The mischievous man must be kept out of mischief, his wings clipped. Whereas you....your wings require nothing less than the sky's infinite expanse.

VAUCANSON: But all the same, do you not find his company anything but trying?

CHATELET: You mean excepting those days of poetry and picnics? Or the evenings in the laboratory? Our coach last year overturned on a freezing winter's night and help had to be sent for.... How did we pass the time? Curled up together in a pile of Russian rugs, identifying the outlines of the lesser constellations....

(We see slides depicting constellations of Delphinus, Cepheus, etc.)

CHATELET: That for one was a beautiful night—

VAUCANSON: It sounds indeed beautiful. *(Brooding—)* Even if you took me as a lover only to spite him...

CHATELET: No Jacques, don't believe it—

VAUCANSON: Even if I am merely a pawn in a lover's quarrel, it has backfired, for I am smitten, utterly, and there isn't a set of calipers in the universe that could measure the length and breadth of it, and I will devote myself to convincing you—

CHATELET: Make this contest then the definitive argument—work and prove Voltaire and his skepticism are misguided....

VAUCANSON: I will Gabrielle, I will, yes, let me show you—

CHATELET: Done then.

VAUCANSON: And perhaps, in the meantime, you should not see the man.

CHATELET: Voltaire? No, I will still see him.

(Beat)

VAUCANSON: So you will still see him?

CHATELET: Yes.

VAUCANSON: I see. So you will still see him then.

CHATELET: Yes.

VAUCANSON: As a friend.

CHATELET: Yes, as a friend.

VAUCANSON: Good. For he is an old friend.

CHATELET: Yes.

VAUCANSON: So as a friend. *(Pause)* And as a lover?

CHATELET: You mustn't fret over such things.

VAUCANSON: I mustn't fret because of course you will not see him as a lover, or I mustn't fret because it will just upset me tremendously?

CHATELET: The latter.

VAUCANSON: The latter.

CHATELET: I have seen him. I am still seeing him, and in fact, he is on his way here as we speak.

VAUCANSON: As we speak?

CHATELET: Yes.

VAUCANSON: As we—how could you invite him here!? Where are my trousers! He is approaching as we speak?! *Mon Dieu!* What do you see in that man!

CHATELET: You have a rare and noble spirit Jacques de Vaucanson.... But he is wittier.

VAUCANSON: For holding nothing sacred he is to be admired?

CHATELET: Perhaps you are right.

VAUCANSON: Perhaps not.

CHATELET: He declared DeMoivre's statement the desperate hope of a febrile old man.

VAUCANSON: He said this? When all of nature argues against it?

CHATELET: He often speaks of you.

VAUCANSON: Does he.

CHATELET: He has great admiration for you.

VAUCANSON: Does he.

(A SERVANT *enters.)*

SERVANT: *Monsieur* Voltaire has arrived.

VAUCANSON: God my god...

CHATELET: You will return to the dancing?

VAUCANSON: No.

CHATELET: Where will you go?

VAUCANSON: I need some air.

CHATELET: He would like to meet you.

VAUCANSON: Yes, and you and all your guests can have fun at my expense. Gabrielle...I can prove him wrong, and if I do succeed, I must know, I must know...will I have your favour? Will you pledge yourself to me alone?

(Pause)

CHATELET: It's likely.

VAUCANSON: That is enough.

CHATELET: *(Handing him peruke)* Take this.

VAUCANSON: I am missing a shoe.

CHATELET: By the window, and please do not be upset.

VAUCANSON: I'm fine I'm fine. But I have to go. Fine then...I'll be off.

CHATELET: Your peruke is crooked.

VAUCANSON: My peruke?

CHATELET: Jacques de Vaucanson, scientist, lover, erupts with an expletive—

VAUCANSON: Fuck my peruke!

CHATELET: Right hand clutches, throws down, peruke, and off he storms, slamming door, leaving peruke.

(VAUCANSON throws down peruke, turns, storms out of room, slams door. Lights up again on ABBE.)

ABBE: So you threw down your peruke...

VAUCANSON: Yes, and I felt great about it. At the time.

ABBE: But what does all that have to do with your ratios?

VAUCANSON: The ratios are in my peruke.

ABBE: Ah, I see. You keep your ratios in your peruke.

VAUCANSON: Yes.

ABBE: And when was this?

VAUCANSON: I don't know...three weeks ago.

ABBE: Well good god man, get them back!

VAUCANSON: *(Tortured)* I can't...I can't...because... no doubt...Voltaire is there as we speak...they are in each other's arms as we speak.... *(Pause. He broods.)* But friend, perhaps you could retrieve my peruke.

ABBE: *(Matter-of-factly, in one sentence—)* I would do anything for you, but you know in this instance that I cannot. I am that man's sworn enemy after I criticized his work on Newton and he denounced me in his pamphlet *Le Preservatif,* and I responded with the stinging condemnation *La Voltairomanie;* and we who once were friends! But of course, he still thinks I should be indebted to him but it is because he is under the mistaken assumption that it was he alone who sprung me from prison after the spurious charge that I corrupted young boys.

VAUCANSON: Damn Damn this peruke. As if I hadn't other things to think about.

ABBE: Do you think it's still in the bedroom?

VAUCANSON: *(Resigned)* Perhaps a servant has carried it away...or thrown it away....

ABBE: *(Alarmed)* Yes, oh christ, or thrown it away. Look, We must take a coach there together immediately—

VAUCANSON: *(Spurred to action)* You'll make inquiries with the servants, and perhaps I can enter the bedroom, if it is unoccupied, via the window...and seek out the curséd hairpiece!

ABBE: We'll find the fastest coach.

VAUCANSON: Until then, every moment is a moment lost.

(The ABBE *and* VAUCANSON *exit. Lights up on Minuet Interlude. Stirring violin, harpsichord.* CHATELET, *dancers.* VAUCANSON *and other characters take their places in minuet.)*

CHATELET: Before we can consider the Minuet, we must consider the complexity and harmony inherent in a single step! We must go Neither fast nor slow—the former is Folly, the latter is Indolence. And Above all, no affectation; the steps must progress naturally, and yet in each step, there is effort, there is premeditation. The knees boldly stretched—The legs slightly turned outward—Head upright, waist steady— With the left arm forward, we advance the right foot... We have begun...

(A knock on VAUCANSON's *door. Door opened tentatively.* LE CAT *enters. Finds no one. Makes himself comfortable. Peruses papers scattered about.* LE CAT *glances at his pocket watch. As diagrams of setting sun, and of rising moon, are projected,* LE CAT *muses—)*

LE CAT: Though standing still, and still as still as it has always stood, the Sun, notwithstanding, steals from view as we pirouette west to east never ceasing never ceasing, and Evening descends as Evening will....

*(*VAUCANSON *enters worse for wear.)*

VAUCANSON: My pardons, I attempted travel this morning only to reach midway and watch the wheel of our carriage fall off and roll away and now the wheel and day are lost...irretrievably....

LE CAT: Monsieur Vaucanson.

VAUCANSON: Do I know you?

LE CAT: You do not. But it is an honor to meet you,
I have heard much of your abilities.

VAUCANSON: How did you get in?

LE CAT: The door was open.

VAUCANSON: No no I locked it.

LE CAT: It was unlocked.

VAUCANSON: It must have been locked.

LE CAT: But it was not.

VAUCANSON: It was locked, surely.

LE CAT: No.

VAUCANSON: But I take pains to secure the door
whene'er I leave.

LE CAT: It was not secured.

VAUCANSON: Are you sure?

LE CAT: I am quite sure.

VAUCANSON: The window perhaps?

LE CAT: I did not come in through the window. Nor did
I spontaneously generate from that plate of meat.

VAUCANSON: I did not wish to suggest that you had.
My pardons if you thought I thought you had
generated spontaneously from that plate of meat.
I suppose the secrecy I cloaked my project in was a
privilege I'd have to relinquish sooner or later. You've
been here long?

LE CAT: Long enough to examine your sketches...
An artificial duck that stretches its neck to take corn
from your hand!

VAUCANSON: *(Growing excited again)* Yes, from the hand! then swallows it greedily, and doubles the swiftness in the motion of its neck and gullet to drive the food into its stomach where it will be digested by dissolution, not trituration as some would have it. The matter digested is conducted by pipes quite to the Anus, where there is a Sphincter that lets it out.

LE CAT: So you have set out to refute De Moivre's statement.

VAUCANSON: No, I have set out to prove De Moivre's statement.

LE CAT: But you are constructing an artificial duck.

VAUCANSON: Yes sir, were you not listening?

LE CAT: If you don't mind my saying so, you will never accomplish it.

VAUCANSON: So far, Courage and Patience have overcome everything. And now if you'll excuse me, I have much work to do, *Monsieur*...I'm sorry, what was your name?

LE CAT: Le Cat.

VAUCANSON: Le Cat? If you are LeCat then you are the most celebrated surgeon in Paris.

LE CAT: I am Le Cat. Now, please, undress, and I shall peruse your penis.

VAUCANSON: You'll what? Ah, You have heard of my adversity.

LE CAT: I have.

VAUCANSON: Madame Du Chatelet recommends you highly, but I cannot afford a doctor.

LE CAT: Do not worry about the cost, for it was *Madame* who sent me here. I was with her this morning.

VAUCANSON: This morning?

LE CAT: Please, your trousers.

VAUCANSON: You were with the *Madame* this morning?

LE CAT: Yes, Monsieur Arouet was distressed at her condition and had me summoned.

VAUCANSON: Monsieur Arouet?

LE CAT: Yes.

VAUCANSON: Francois Arouet?

LE CAT: Yes.

VAUCANSON: By Francois Arouet you mean of course Voltaire?

LE CAT: Yes.

VAUCANSON: He was there was he...Voltaire...

(VAUCANSON, *trouserless, picks up a very large book and reads a page to hide his thoughts while* LE CAT *speaks*)

LE CAT: Oh yes, they are much in love. I don't usually believe in such tripe but you can feel it in the air, their love...

VAUCANSON: Fine.

LE CAT: And early this morning he was alarmed to find *Madame* suffering from great swoons and any amount of vomit.

VAUCANSON: My God is she all right?

LE CAT: In a manner of speaking. She is pregnant.

VAUCANSON: *(To self, with delight)* Great swoons...and any amount of vomit...are two reactions contemplated then suppressed by this scientist upon hearing the news of a pump beating in tiny two-four counterpoint to the greater pump above it and all this occurred in the time it took for a large book to slip from the hands and fall at a velocity proportional not to its weight but to the time elapsed in its falling.

LE CAT: *(Rewinding to previous line:)* In a manner of speaking. She is pregnant.

(The book falls from the hands of VAUCANSON *with a thud)*

VAUCANSON: I see.

LE CAT: Yes, and true to her nature, she said never mind her, she would foot the bill if I went straight away to the studios of the suffering Jacques de Vaucanson.

VAUCANSON: *(Failing to disguise excitement)* But this is...this is staggering....

LE CAT: Is it.

VAUCANSON: ...How truly...miraculous...for her....

LE CAT: Yes, well Shall we get on? If you may, please bend from the waist to eighty-five degrees.

VAUCANSON: *(Bending)* A child... Well!... *(Ready to compute—)* ...And how pregnant is she?

LE CAT: There is another eight months before the infant receives the first of many rude shocks.

VAUCANSON: Eight months....yes, that would do it....amazing....amazing....a tiny life....

LE CAT: Well you seem certainly more moved by the event than Voltaire.

VAUCANSON: *(Sobered by possibility of paternal rival)* Oh yes, Voltaire. *(Testing)* How did he take the news?

LE CAT: I can't say favorably. After all, in less than a month, *Madame*'s husband is expected home from the military campaigns in Corsica—

VAUCANSON: *(Still more sobered)* Oh yes, her husband...

LE CAT: *(Examining rectal area)* There's quite a scar
I see.... You've had surgery before?

VAUCANSON: Three years ago.

LE CAT: It's a perilous operation. One's chances of
survival are quite small.

VAUCANSON: That fact was made known to me
only afterward. How close...how close I came to
obliteration....And all for a stone.

LE CAT: A trivial death is the most appropriate sort of
death for it does not obscure, nay in fact it underscores,
the irrefutable insignificance of individual life. Don't
you agree?

VAUCANSON: No I do not, and the stone they removed
was the size of a tennis ball.

LE CAT: I don't doubt it.

VAUCANSON: And I still pass gravel in my urine.
No, never the knife again.

LE CAT: Well, if you change your mind, I have
developed techniques that avoid many of the
complications caused by this sort of surgery in the past.

VAUCANSON: What sort of complications?

LE CAT: Well, sterility for one.

(Pause)

VAUCANSON: Sterility?

LE CAT: You were made aware that a procedure like the
one you endured almost always results in sterility.

VAUCANSON: *(Devastated)* Sterility. No. No I was not
made aware.

LE CAT: Do you have children?

VAUCANSON: Do I have children?

(A slide is projected—a lateral view of the male reproductive system with penis)

LE CAT: It's a lateral cut of the perineum to reach the urethra, where the stone is impacted, and the slightest slip of the knife will sever the *vas deferens* which connects to it.

VAUCANSON: *(Profound dejection)* And the *vas deferens* carries the juice of the testicles.

LE CAT: Yes. I'm sorry to have to tell you but it's a near certainty. I thought you knew...

VAUCANSON: *(Half to self)* ...and we can be reasonably assured then that Voltaire has not the same curse upon him....

LE CAT: I should say he has amply proved otherwise.

VAUCANSON: ...no little chicks...and my life will end with me...and all that will live on... *(Taking solace)* ...is my work.

LE CAT: And all because from the same tube men emit both waste and life...which perhaps is why waste and life are so difficult to distinguish from one another.

VAUCANSON: You say so, but I do not think so.

LE CAT: You do not think so, but think of Needham, who through the tube of his microscope witnessed in a teardrop the swarming of little eels so small that a cluster of a million could not be discerned by the human eye. A cluster of a million! And no doubt this universe is but another teardrop, containing all of mankind and all his great grand history besides. Blot it up with a handkerchief and who, pray tell, will take notice?

VAUCANSON: You may well ask!

LE CAT: I needn't ask, for I know the answer. No one. And no thing.

VAUCANSON: No sir, no sir, no event goes unfelt, and even the flap of wings on a gnat now dead may no doubt be amplified through space and time into a thunderclap, for all things are ineluctably connected—

LE CAT: I assure you sir, the stars stand aloof, and so do I.

VAUCANSON: You can try, but I tell you not a particle in the universe can make such a claim, much less a surgeon—

LE CAT: —One who sees all this soup of living and dying for what it is—a dish of laughable insignificance.

VAUCANSON: There is nothing laughable and nothing insignificant. Do you not see that in the infinite chain of beings, our earth, our body, are among the necessary links? In every droplet of sea water you'll find Needham's little eels. Look and you'll see the movement of one little eel affecting and affected by other little eels, and other little eels still other little eels, until the entire droplet is affected, and each droplet affecting other countless droplets until it is the very sea that is affected, yes the sea, that engenders clouds, and the clouds that furnish the rain that nourishes the earth that binds the moon that makes the tides that affects the ships, and sailors on ships, and the wives of those sailors on ships and the handkerchiefs of those wives waved at departing sailors on ships, and the teardrops in those handkerchiefs and the eels in those tear drops, the eels sir, the eels sir... To say nothing of the sailors' wives' grandfathers' uncles!—

LE CAT: To say nothing is right! You have said nothing as to the purpose of it all. To what end?

VAUCANSON: That we will discover in time, and in the meantime we have this... (Searching for word) ...this dance.... And there is no begging out of it—you say you stand aloof, but a man who says he has left a ballroom has done nothing of the sort. He has merely stepped outside and under the stars and into an even greater, all-encompassing, incomparable Minuet.

LE CAT: A Minuet. If this Universe is a dance, sir, it is nothing more than the spasmodic dance of a boy who has just burned his tongue.

VAUCANSON: *(The gracious host)* Yes, well, thank you doctor. Now if you don't mind, I have much work—

LE CAT: I have some suggested courses of treatment—

VAUCANSON: Thank you all the same, but I'm not interested, you can tell Madame Chatelet I said as much—

LE CAT: Madame Chatelet, yes, I nearly forgot— she sent this on to give to you.

(LE CAT *hands* VAUCANSON *his peruke)*

VAUCANSON: My peruke! Say what you will Le Cat, but I will prove all your doubts wrong with this!

LE CAT: With your peruke?

(But VAUCANSON *realizes the ratios are not to be found)*

VAUCANSON: Le Cat, did you not perhaps from this wig see slip a slip of paper as you traveled from Chatelet's?

LE CAT: No.

(Pause)

VAUCANSON: No matter... No matter. But if you would be so good as to survey your carriage.

LE CAT: Of course. May I ask what the slip contained?

VAUCANSON: Merely...effort.

LE CAT: It occurs to me that as I was riding here I espied a spider within your peruke and I shook the peruke violently outside the window, dislodging the spider—

VAUCANSON: —and perhaps the paper—

LE CAT: It is possible.

VAUCANSON: Where was this?

LE CAT: Some miles between Paris and Cirey on the King's Highway.

VAUCANSON: Can you be more specific?

LE CAT: No.

VAUCANSON: Right, fine, thank you. I will show you now the door—

LE CAT: Thank you all the same but I can find it myself. I wouldn't recommend across this floor any unclad feet.... (*Notices toes of* VAUCANSON *poking through large holes in his stockings*) My dear sir, your feet—

VAUCANSON: Yes.

LE CAT: They're webbed.

VAUCANSON: An incomplete separation of the digits. My father's feet were the same.

LE CAT: Were they.... And his father's before him?

VAUCANSON: I don't know.

LE CAT: Because it is a trait known to pass from one generation to the next.

VAUCANSON: Is it?

LE CAT: But of course, Sterile Sam, the trait will end with you.

VAUCANSON: (*Through gritted teeth*) Yes. It will end with me. And now the door—

LE CAT: Webbed feet. So that is why you've set out to construct of all things, a clockwork duck.

VAUCANSON: No, actually...that hadn't occurred to me....

LE CAT: Come sir, surely——

VAUCANSON: No, it is coincidence.

LE CAT: Pure accident! And here you are constructing a duck to prove there is no such thing! How then did you fix upon the idea specifically of a duck?

VAUCANSON: *(Suspicious)* Do you really want to know?

LE CAT: I do.

(We hear crickets, frogs, distant ducks, and see perhaps a projection "3 weeks previous")

VAUCANSON: *(Carrying shoes)* How the sky was awash with stars that night of the ball at du Chatelet's chateau.... It was about three weeks ago, I was in a disagreeable mood, I needed air, but just as I was taking my leave for the evening I was foolishly convinced in participating in that vexatious game wherein all the shoes of all the guests are piled in one enormous pile, and when all was said and done, I wound up with shoes that resembled mine in every respect except they were too small by half. As I roamed the grounds wet with dew—

(We hear the sound of a man vomiting into a body of water)

VAUCANSON: I heard coming from the banks of the pond—

(More vomiting, and LAZARRO SPALLANZANI is revealed. Pitiful groans heard from the man as well. Italian accent, clearly exhausting for him to communicate with VAUCANSON, and a struggle for VAUCANSON as well. By end of scene however, they are finishing each other's sentences.)

VAUCANSON: The punch at Madame du Chatelet's gatherings tends to be quite strong.

SPALLANZANI: I cannot-a speak-a French.

VAUCANSON: You are Italian.

SPALLANZANI: Yes, so...how you say...shove off.

VAUCANSON: My pardons. Never mind.

SPALLANZANI: But what is it that you said. I must try. I must try.

VAUCANSON: Merely that you've had too much to drink....

SPALLANZANI: No, no, I never drink! It is...the after-effects....

VAUCANSON: Yes?

SPALLANZANI: of...what is the word...oh to hell with it.

VAUCANSON: No, no, What? You must try. The after-effects of what.

SPALLANZANI: The after-effects of...experiments I performed on-a myself.

VAUCANSON: Experiments? For the contest sponsored by the Royal Academy?

SPALLANZANI: No. The contest, it has-a been made public?

VAUCANSON: It hasn't, but perhaps you had gotten wind—

SPALLANZANI: I do not have-a wind! But you found out this contest? From whom?

VAUCANSON: I have only just now been informed by Madame du Chatelet.

SPALLANZANI: Ah, they say-a she is a most-a remarkable woman.

VAUCANSON: She is...most remarkable.... *(Aside)* And what with Voltaire having just returned, I for now must extinguish all thought of her, or I will surely torment myself to oblivion.

SPALLANZANI: *(Half to self)* Why I am here? I would not be missed if I left.

VAUCANSON: Were you not invited?

SPALLANZANI: No. Yes. I mean France. This...Earth.

VAUCANSON: *(Encouragingly)* I hear there will be fireworks later.

SPALLANZANI: The fireworks will never come.... How do you say in French.... How-a vain-a is all-a human thought!

VAUCANSON: Your French is sound, but not your conclusion.

SPALLANZANI: How-a petty is all our ideas!

VAUCANSON: You are overwrought.

SPALLANZANI: Petty! And How-a poor our glories and-a all our labors!

VAUCANSON: No. Shush!

(Pause)

SPALLANZANI: How-a wretched we are!

VAUCANSON: Quiet.

(Pause)

SPALLANZANI: Wretched.

VAUCANSON: No. Cease and I will tell you the topic of this year's contest.

SPALLANZANI: I am very sick.

(While Spallanzani retches with volume and violence, Vaucanson recites:)

VAUCANSON: The contest is thus.
Prove or refute the following statement:
The Apparent Randomness of Events in Nature
Will, if subjected to Calculation,
Reveal an underlying Order
Expressing Exquisite Wisdom and Design

SPALLANZANI: I did not get any of that. Once more please.

VAUCANSON: The Apparent... Oh what's the point...

SPALLANZANI: No no, you must tell me...you must try....

VAUCANSON: *(Miming/gesturing as best he can, but ridiculously)* The Apparent Randomness of Events in Nature—

SPALLANZANI: The apparent randomness...

VAUCANSON: *(Miming)* Yes— Will, If Subjected to Calculation,

SPALLANZANI: yes...

VAUCANSON: *(Miming)* Reveal an Underlying Order

SPALLANZANI: An Underlying Order—

VAUCANSON: *(Miming)* Expressing Exquisite Wisdom and Design. Prove or refute.

SPALLANZANI: Ah yes, and tell me, will you prove or refute?

VAUCANSON: Prove.

SPALLANZANI: How.

VAUCANSON: *(Clutching* SPALLANZANI*)* I don't know, but I must...*must* think of something, Everything depends on it!

SPALLANZANI: Tonight my mood is black, yes, but I don't see how it can be done without much deceit.

VAUCANSON: No, I cannot believe that.

SPALLANZANI: It is all foul and pointless endeavorings. Instead of vomiting into this duck pond, I should drown myself in it. But the problem...is that I can swim, and I would swim through the muck and the lilypad back-a to the edge despite myself, yes? It makes-a no sense, why I should cling to this...dunghill.

VAUCANSON: You are feeling low after a failed experiment, that is all. I have often felt the same way.

SPALLANZANI: I don't care! But...perhaps.

VAUCANSON: What experiment were you working on before being forced to abandon it?

SPALLANZANI: *(Becoming animated)* It concerned-a...Life!

VAUCANSON: Excellent!

SPALLANZANI: How inert matter somehow becomes flesh.

VAUCANSON: For instance?

SPALLANZANI: *(With heavy accent)* Sémen-a.

VAUCANSON: What?

SPALLANZANI: Sémen-a.

VAUCANSON: *(Not getting it)* One more time.

SPALLANZANI: Sémen-a!

VAUCANSON: One more time.

SPALLANZANI: Sémen-a!

(Pause)

VAUCANSON: *(Straining)* One more time.

SPALLANZANI: Oh to hell with it.

VAUCANSON: *(Timidly trying again)* Sémena?

SPALLANZANI: I said forget it!

VAUCANSON: Fine.

SPALLANZANI: *(Under breath)* To hell with everyone.

VAUCANSON: I'm sorry?

SPALLANZANI: I said to hell with you!

VAUCANSON: Well to hell with you!

SPALLANZANI: Just-a leave me alone, eh? I want to be just-a with the lilypads and the frogs.

VAUCANSON: Fine. You have your liberty. The croaking's too loud for me anyway.

SPALLANZANI: They are seeking mates.

VAUCANSON: *(Walking away, to self—)* And they'll find nothing but heartache and despair—

SPALLANZANI: The female frog, she lays her twenty thousand eggs, and the male sprays his sémen-a on top of them, and in one week, tadpoles.

VAUCANSON: *(Stops, now realizing)* ...semen... Semen!

SPALLANZANI: Yes! Yes! Sémena! Inert matter! And in one week, tadpoles! How? How is this possible?

VAUCANSON: Yes— How indeed. What is it in the semen that creates life?

SPALLANZANI: No one knows, but I can tell you that it is the same for both man and frog.

VAUCANSON: Ah but look here, man is not a frog.

SPALLANZANI: Is man not a frog?

VAUCANSON: I say to you Man is not a Frog.

SPALLANZANI: The difference, it is trivial.

(Duck quack and frog croak at minimum volume)

VAUCANSON: I don't know his name, but Impulses from the gastrointestinal tract of my fellow scientist have been sent to his brain. The brain then sends back impulses that precipitate spasmodic muscular contractions. The pressure generated forces up the contents of his stomach, namely: bile, three prunes and a dollop of porridge.

SPALLANZANI: I do not-a know his name, but in the pelvis of this fellow, the muscular sac, holding a half a pint of urine, is irritated by a calcium concretion floating in the urine, and suddenly begins persistent-a rigid contractions.

(*Beat. Then* VAUCANSON *is attacked by an intense bladder spasm, and almost simultaneously,* SPALLANZANI *begins retching with violence and misery. Quite Prolonged.* VAUCANSON *attempts to stifle pain and prevent from urinating, while desperately attempting to undo his trousers but a button becomes stuck. He rolls on ground, he stands up again, fighting with button. Frog croak and duck quack quite voluble.*)

VAUCANSON: (*With violence*) I can't undo the button! Come button! Cursed button!

(SPALLANZANI, *retching now waning, has collapsed on ground, and crawls toward* VAUCANSON. VAUCANSON *has sudden realization that his bladder is emptying into his trousers.*)

VAUCANSON: Oh God... (*He sinks to ground*)

SPALLANZANI: Your pants, they are damp.

VAUCANSON: You see a man in trousers humiliated.

SPALLANZANI: Do not be embarrassed.

VAUCANSON: This wretched wretched bladder...
I'd sooner not eat or drink anything again—

SPALLANZANI: No, no....We eat and we grow into men.

VAUCANSON: (*Stimulated*) Ah, again—inert matter into living matter—

SPALLANZANI: Yes, food! That is it. In our stomach...
a...a...

VAUCANSON: Yes, yes...a...a..

SPALLANZANI: A...how you say—

VAUCANSON: a...a...Transubstantiation!

SPALLANZANI: A what?

VAUCANSON: Food into flesh—

SPALLANZANI: That is good—

VAUCANSON: These were the experiments you
conducted?

SPALLANZANI: My rival Reaumur, damn him, he
persuaded a duck to swallow a sponge that the duck
then regurgitated.

VAUCANSON: Go on.

SPALLANZANI: But are the juices in the human-a
stomach like those in other beasts? That is the question.
So I myself swallowed not just a sponge, but many-a
bags of chemicals.

VAUCANSON: You showed admirable conviction—

SPALLANZANI: But I could not vomit them up again!
Reaumur's duck, he could, that god-damn duck , he
could and I could not. And now I think the packets
have broken open for I vomit all the time, and with
blood.

VAUCANSON: I have seen a human carnival performer
who swallowed stones for a living and then regurgitate
them at will. You might have hired someone like him to
swallow your packets.

(Pause)

SPALLANZANI: I did not think of that.

VAUCANSON: Nevertheless, yours was a worthy experiment.

SPALLANZANI: And yet I am sure I would find the gastric juices similar between man and duck.

VAUCANSON: But look here, man is not a duck.

SPALLANZANI: Is man not a duck?

VAUCANSON: I say to you Man is not a Duck.

SPALLANZANI: The difference, it is trivial.

VAUCANSON: No. Our nobility, our reason, puts us in a different class altogether from the duck...

SPALLANZANI: And yet...look...look at one of those creatures...

(SPALLANZANI *points at duck by pond, we hear gentle quacking*)

SPALLANZANI: See! It walks, it flutters its wings, it feels irritations—

VAUCANSON: Yes, you're right, it runs away, it comes back again—

SPALLANZANI: —it-a makes a complaining sound, yes? It feels pain—

VAUCANSON: —it shows affection—

SPALLANZANI: —it has desires, it gets-a pleasure from this or that....

(*Music more stirring, up on frogs and ducks*)

VAUCANSON: Yes you're right, it certainly shows all the emotions that you show!

(*Music more stirring still*)

SPALLANZANI: And it eats and eliminates just as you do!

VAUCANSON: Better than I do!

SPALLANZANI: And here they say that it has-a no soul—that it's just a machine—

VAUCANSON: *(A realization begins to coalesce) A machine? Oh no my friend, it is—*

SPALLANZANI: No, that spark of life, it will never be explained.

VAUCANSON: We do not know it yet, but do not call that unknowable. Good god sir, are we not scientists? There were mysteries all around us that we...we have exploded! The formulas for that duck may be more complex than those of a clock—

SPALLANZANI: Hah! A hundred million billion times more complex—

VAUCANSON: —fine! Yes! But a hundred million billion is still a *finite* number, of course it is! And therefore, with time, attainable. I assure you sir, we are living equations —

SPALLANZANI: —machines then—

VAUCANSON: —but *how exquisite the Design....*

(Music now shimmering, inspiring—)

SPALLANZANI: *(Clutching* VAUCANSON's *shoulders, with tears)* My god...it is true...it is true!....*Signore,* we are living in a utopia...

VAUCANSON: *(Clutching* SPALLANZANI, *with tears)* I know...I know, my friend....

SPALLANZANI: —under this canopy of stars...

VAUCANSON: —aneath the music and whirrings of the spheres, it is truly—

SPALLANZANI: —the best of all—

VAUCANSON: —possible worlds—

SPALLANZANI: —where even those ducks—

VAUCANSON: —yes, those excreting ducks by a stagnant pond are —

SPALLANZANI: —a glorious necessity—

VAUCANSON: —and contain within their atoms—

SPALLANZANI: —the blueprint—

VAUCANSON: —of the universe!... *(Growing excited at a thought forming in head—)* ....indeed....indeed—

SPALLANZANI: *(Pointing to the ground, ecstatic)* —Holy God, Signore—You have-a my shoes!

(Music still more stirring, and fireworks begin to be set off. A great booming, and slides of flares)

VAUCANSON: *(Ecstatic, clutching Spallanzani even tighter, and completing thought—)* Nothing is random! ...Nothing is random, and I will prove it! ...Employing Newton's laws of attraction by which the tides behave and the planets are known to rotate; Using calculations plotting the movement of the stars themselves across the heavens; Utilizing a system of springs and weights, gearwheels, cogs and escapements of my own construction fashioned in ratios of proven mathematical laws and proportion...I will create a Duck,,,,that flaps its wings, eats, and excretes...just like a duck!

(Musical coda. The slides change to another picture. SPALLANZANI *has exited.)*

VAUCANSON: Any questions?

(It becomes clear that VAUCANSON *is now in the midst of a fund-raising presentation. The* ABBE *is assisting with the Magic Lantern slides.)*

CITIZEN #1: Why a duck?

VAUCANSON: I believe I have just explained to you why a duck.

CITIZEN #2: It is a clockwork.

VAUCANSON: Yes.

CITIZEN #2: Will it tell the time?

VAUCANSON: Of course not! But! Study the movement of the humerus in the wing and you will observe the same mathematical ratios that send Mars around the Sun, watch the duck stretch out its neck and you are witnessing the formulae that predict the curl of smoke from a pipe, steam from a kettle, the shape of a cumulus cloud or a plume of dust from a cart, in short, you will observe chaos itself made sensical by mathematical principles!

CITIZEN #3: Good God, you are creating the universe—

CITIZEN #2: What you propose sir is impossible!

VAUCANSON: Impossible?

CITIZEN #2: Of course you do not want to hear such an opinion.

VAUCANSON: No, no...tell me the things that are not possible, for those are the things that I will do...I require a minimum of funding and your names shall be attached to an undertaking that will be spoken of centuries hence!

(Montage, with much music. We see VAUCANSON *hard at work, e.g. filing gears, tearing down designs from the wall, crippled by bladder spasms. We then see projected a landscape, with a road stretching on. We hear bird whistle, and the lowing of cows)*

ABBE: How large is this strip of paper?

VAUCANSON: Yea long.

(Pause)

ABBE: And you propose we should walk yet a mile further on this road in search of it?

VAUCANSON: Have we a choice? I can little believe that such ratios, so vital to this work, nay, essential to the completion of it, will not return to my possession.

(Long pause)

ABBE: But Jacques, the odds....

VAUCANSON: Blast the odds! Odds are irrelevant! This duck was meant to be made!

ABBE: I say.... *(Spying scrap of paper on ground)* Jacques! Jacques!

(They dive for the scrap. VAUCANSON *reads scrap.)*

VAUCANSON: *(Disappointed)* No, it is not the ratios. It appears to be a strip torn from a love letter.

ABBE: Here on the king's highway?

VAUCANSON: It was a blustery day on November 12th. Perhaps in a man's hand is pressed a letter from his Love just as he is taking his leave. In his carriage he reads with great anticipation, but finds that instead of cooing phrases, she is calling it off. "Enough," she writes. "I wish it done." The man shreds the letter and scatters it to the wind, and here a scrap descended, to lie befouled....in a ditch....

ABBE: Well that's certainly one possibility. *(Concerned by* VAUCANSON'*s narrative)* Jacques... How fares Madame Chatelet?

VAUCANSON: I wouldn't know.

ABBE: You have not heard from her?

VAUCANSON: I have not. Nor have I thought of her. *(Pause)* I never think of her.

(Thunder rumbles. A storm begins.)

ABBE: *(Hopeful that they can now go home)* Shall we give up?

(Pause. The rain falls hard.)

VAUCANSON: No!

*(Thunder claps. Montage continues. Much music.
We see VAUCANSON building the framework,
studying the movements of makeshift wings, drinking
turpentine, running over list of more materials needed.)*

VAUCANSON: Read it back to me.

ABBE: *(Reading)* "One worm gear with a hundred
and twelve toothed wheel and threaded cylinder,
two-pint-eight inch diameter, twenty feet of copper
wire, eleven pound torque, and additional amounts
for the cubitus of the right wing. Also feathers. Mallard.

VAUCANSON: Good.

ABBE: But you have not found the ratios?

VAUCANSON: I will have to reconstruct them.

ABBE: Do you have time?

VAUCANSON: Plenty. If I do not sleep.

*(Montage continues, with VAUCANSON tearing down
designs from the wall, crippled by bladder spasms, fighting
sleep, finally falling asleep. Darkness. We then hear, softly,
CHATELET singing the opening song. Lights up.
VAUCANSON, at table, head resting on palm, slowly awakes,
and singing softly next to him, an eight-month pregnant
CHATELET.)*

VAUCANSON: You?

CHATELET: You.

VAUCANSON: Am I awake?

CHATELET: I promise.

VAUCANSON: ...I dreamt...I don't even remember,
except I stood naked with months of work for naught
and a deadline in less than a day...

CHATELET: No, you have still nearly a month.... And you will shape infinity into the dimensions of a duck.

VAUCANSON: But my dream, so vivid... All that work... and no indication that they were all calculations in futility—

CHATELET: Dreams are for the dead.... You can dream...but you can do more than dream—

VAUCANSON: Yes, I can make a duck drink, play in the water with his bill, and unleash a gurgling noise like a real living duck...but with no assurance that I will not awake and find it was all yet again for naught—

CHATELET: Then awake and begin again, so long as you find yourself awake—strive! What more can you do?

VAUCANSON: With every atom of my being, I love you...I love you, and I know *how* all things move, yes, but *what* is it that moves them? What? And suddenly I am convinced that it is this love for you. For without you, all the world would seem lifeless and inanimate, I know it. But if I know the how and what, I still will never know why.... Why do all things move and why do I persist in loving you when you are clearly in love with someone else and carrying his child?

CHATELET: Jacques de Vaucanson....Why do you think I've come to you? Because I have decided at long last to choose the man whose vision offers mankind a glimpse of things to come....

VAUCANSON: *(Looks around the room, then realizes—)* Me?

CHATELET: There are many who say what you are attempting cannot be done—

VAUCANSON: So many raspberries have been blown at me, the air is fragrant with fruit—

CHATELET: And yet you have faith...and I don't want to live with someone without it...the faith that all

humanity tries as hard as it can, that we all mean
well...that History may prove us wrong, but we did
what we thought best, with what we had—

VAUCANSON: Yes... Faith. It is slow but I know progress
comes daily even though I cannot see it.... But how
maddening in its pace.

CHATELET: Everything, from the wing of a dragonfly
to the invention of the harpsichord, everything,
everything, everything was built on trial and error.

VAUCANSON: Yes, yes it's true—

CHATELET: —from the powder in your peruke to
Newton's First Law of Motion—

VAUCANSON: Yes.

CHATELET: The door hinge, and the pendulum clock.

VAUCANSON: And domestic livestock breeding.

CHATELET: And soap-manufacturing—

VAUCANSON: —and knowledge of the lymphatic
system—

*(By now a bit of intellectual/romantic play between them,
which brings them closer)*

CHATELET: —and stained glass—

VAUCANSON: —double-entry bookkeeping—

CHATELET: —and the Gregorian calendar.

VAUCANSON: The cultivation of the cabernet grape—

CHATELET: —intercolumniation—

VAUCANSON: —and the moldboard plough—

CHATELET: —and the bagpipes.

VAUCANSON: And dephlogisticated air.

CHATELET: Plus the banquet couch—

VAUCANSON: —and belaying pins on ships.

CHATELET: And the parasol—

VAUCANSON: —the flintlock—

CHATELET: —bobbin lace—

VAUCANSON: —the crosstitch—

CHATELET: —the mapping of Africa—

VAUCANSON: —and the shoemaker's awl for pegging shoes!

CHATELET: Yes.

VAUCANSON: They all came about through struggle—

CHATELET: *(By now in embrace—)* —so Patience. Mankind is still in its infancy.

VAUCANSON: Yes—

CHATELET: I have faith in you...have patience with me and we will construct a life together—

VAUCANSON: *(Beginning to feel giddy)* Upon trial and error—

CHATELET: Yes.

VAUCANSON: And you truly mean it.

CHATELET: Not only do I mean it, I'm quite o'erwhelmed by it—

VAUCANSON: *(Beaming for first time in play)* You're quite o'erwhelmed? How...most...excellent good.

CHATELET: And Jacques perhaps, perhaps the child is yours...

VAUCANSON: No no no, it's not, it's not...but no matter...I don't mind....

(Pause)

CHATELET: Well...I should go...

VAUCANSON: I want to be with you.

CHATELET: No, I mustn't stand in your way....but such days ahead...*(They kiss)* ...I can taste them on my lips...

VAUCANSON: *(Tears of happiness)* yes....yes....

CHATELET: *(Nearly exiting, then turning around and saying matter-of-factly)* Oh, I nearly forgot. I found this scrap of paper in my bedroom. I don't know if its important. It appears to contain a number of different ratios....and its in your handwriting.... Have you been looking for it?

(V AUCANSON seizes scrap of paper. Montage with still grander music. V AUCANSON in untucked shirt, wrench clenched in teeth, tearing down designs from the wall, bending duck prototype with pliers, etc. Musical coda, then a number of insistent knocks on the door. V AUCANSON is deeply engrossed in hard thought and pained study and intense labor.)

ABBE: *(Through door)* Jacques...Jacques, it is I —

VAUCANSON: It's open.

ABBE: It's not open.

(Pause. Then knock knock knock)

VAUCANSON: It's open.

ABBE: Jacques it's locked.

VAUCANSON: It isn't. You have to push.

ABBE: I am. I am pushing.

VAUCANSON: No, push....push.

ABBE: I'm pushing.

VAUCANSON: Hold the handle and push.

ABBE: For God's sake, it is locked.

VAUCANSON: It is not locked. I was occasioned to unlock it an hour ago!

(Pause. More knocking. Pause)

ABBE: Jacques. The door is locked.

VAUCANSON: I'm telling you it's open, stop knocking and push.

ABBE: Jacques, we don't have much time—

VAUCANSON: *(Half to self)* I know...I know...in less than ninety-six hours I'm to present to the Academy a deterministic, dynamic model that yet will elucidate irregular, unpredictable behavior...

(Pause)

ABBE: What? Jacques, I can't hear you.... Look, I have news of grave import that perhaps you have not heard, I beg of you, open the—

(VAUCANSON pulls on door, unfastens bolt, opens door.)

VAUCANSON: Who continues to lock my door against my wishes?! Everywhere I turn, unexpected impediments!

(The ABBE looks distraught, despite efforts to hide it. Though also clear that he is no longer the sot he was at beginning of play.)

ABBE: You look terrible.

VAUCANSON: The work...The work involved!

ABBE: There's food outside the door—

VAUCANSON: Leave it outside.

ABBE: *(Retrieving it)* You must try to eat a little.

VAUCANSON: I cannot.

ABBE: When was the last time you ate?

VAUCANSON: I don't remember. I can't even look at it.

ABBE: It is nourishment.

VAUCANSON: Put it out of sight.

ABBE: *(Putting it behind screen)* If you want it, it's over here.

VAUCANSON: Fine.

ABBE: Do you see? Over here.

VAUCANSON: Fine! Now what is this about news of grave import...

ABBE: Yes...I will come to that. Jacques, how are you proceedng?

VAUCANSON: I don't know if it's progress, or if I'm just going in circles. I haven't left my rooms for weeks. So many different moving parts in such a small automaton—

ABBE: I'm worried about you, Jacques, sleep—there's such a thing as that—

VAUCANSON: Do you know where mankind would be if he always got a proper night's sleep? Still in the mud! We are the only creature who has said, "I am tired, but until I am finished, I will not sleep" — I will not sleep—

(A knock on the door. The ABBE opens it to reveal LE CAT.)

LE CAT: Abbe, you are here? So you have told him?

ABBE: No...I have not told him.

VAUCANSON: Told me what?

(Silence. A pause long enough for VAUCANSON, and perhaps audience too, to understand fully that CHATELET has died in childbirth.)

VAUCANSON: Oh god....

LE CAT: You could feed all the pigs in all the farms in France I'd wager from the trough containing nothing but our hard-won knowledge...And I think the pigs wouldn't notice a whit of difference between it and their usual fodder....

VAUCANSON: I disagree.

LE CAT: The ultimate cause of things has no more regard to good above ill than to heat above cold—

VAUCANSON: No, I disagree. But tell me Abbe, why was I not informed—

ABBE: I was summoned by Madame du Chatelet to be present, for she was enduring a labor long and difficult but your work she did not want to disturb.

VAUCANSON: How did Voltaire receive the news?

ABBE: He is in bed, having fallen down the stairs. His servant attests that he saw his master throw himself down on purpose....

VAUCANSON: The child?

ABBE: ...A girl... It struggled til morning, then it too....

LE CAT: And so we see our man's seed, hell-bent on producing life, has instead produced nothing but death....I once asserted that a trivial death had the most befitting irony...but a death in childbirth quite eclipses it.

VAUCANSON: You say these things out of fear Le Cat.

LE CAT: Cynicism. I have seen too much of the world to feel otherwise.

VAUCANSON: And that assertion is uttered out of naivete...for contrary to your belief you have not seen enough to know...to know truly the way of things—

LE CAT: I have seen enough to know that life is little more than the momentary difficulty when swallowing your slaver.

VAUCANSON: No.

LE CAT: It gives one nothing but nausea to see you stand here and say that our lady's death was all part of God's shimmering plan—

VAUCANSON: *(Obviously struggling heroically with grief)* Her death...Madame du Chatelet's...death...so as her life...has and will continue to have generated incalculable consequences, and the world is altered irrevocably for her having lived in it, and died in it, just as the world had been influenced and adjusted step by step again and again before our time until it produced, as one of its near-innumerable effects, a child who would become Gabrielle-Emilie, patroness of the Sciences, and she might have perished when she was three, before anyone knew her or loved her, she might have succumbed to smallpox or consumption, or been run down by a carriage, or had her brains dashed out by a Hessian soldier when but a girl but it was not til now and it was this and so—

LE CAT: —And so we will not find you throwing yourself down stairs?

VAUCANSON: No. Now If you will excuse me doctor, I have much work—

LE CAT: I should say you do. Tell me... What did you mean....that I said what I said out of fear?

VAUCANSON: What is your fear, Le Cat? The fear of striving for not a scrap of recompense...The fear that all the faithless share—that you will never find meaning in your loves and labours, so why even attempt...

LE CAT: *(Profoundly sobered)* Yes....perhaps you are right....I am...moved by your vision, Jacques de Vaucanson, the magnitude of your undertaking... your fortitude.... You are a bulwark....a bulwark... and I thank you for it....I thank you for it.... *(He exits)*

VAUCANSON: Abbe....Was there much suffering?

ABBE: *(Lying)* No. All in all she succumbed most peaceably....But where then do you stand with the project, Jacques....Will you wash your hands of it?

VAUCANSON: Abandon the work?

ABBE: Perhaps you should give up.

VAUCANSON: No, no surely you understand the sincere necessity of completing it.

ABBE: I am relieved. Is there anything you need?

VAUCANSON: This is a list. The last.

ABBE: I'll go then. And Jacques...thank you...

VAUCANSON: Thank you?

ABBE: You, and who would have thought it, but you have replenished my faith in God. *(Exiting)* May your endeavor be blessed my son.

VAUCANSON: Abbe... Were there any last words...

ABBE: None to speak of. Madame du Chatelet's last words were regarding her child—

VAUCANSON: The daughter.

ABBE: Yes.

VAUCANSON: Abbe...*was* there much suffering?

ABBE: Yes. Much.

VAUCANSON: What were the words?

ABBE: She shook out of her delirium long enough to ask, "*Et comment ça va mon petit canard?*" She expired soon after.

VAUCANSON: "*Petit Canard*"...why *canard*? Why a duck?

ABBE: *(Unaware of full significance)* Barely noticeable, but the child's toes were incompletely separated... lending an appearance of webbing.

(Stirring music. In silhouette, we see a representation of VAUCANSON's *duck, slowly moving. The duck sits atop a platform, underneath of which is a vast complex network of gears, levers, cylinders, etc.)*

MEMBER OF ACADEMY: We will never fully know the obstacles this great man has overcome to construct such a—

CITIZEN #2: It is an object of wonderment—

CITIZEN #3: That he will be made a full member of the Academy, that is certain!

CITIZEN #4: It must tour Europe—

CITIZEN #2: It will be the inspiration and awe of the continent—

CITIZEN #4: And England, birthplace of Isaac Newton—

CITIZEN #3: When once wound up, the machine performs all its different operations without being touched again—

ABBE: I will provide you an in-depth description of the movements of the duck, including the random stammer—

MEMBER OF ACADEMY: It is the Greatest Proof Yet Constructed that there is Wisdom and Design behind all Creation!

VAUCANSON: *(To self, still in shock)* Dreams are for the dead, and while you are awake...strive....

CITIZEN #4: *(With tears)* That is not merely a duck up on that pedestal, it is Mankind, it is all of us, our lives.... He has captured the very essence of Human Existence!

VAUCANSON: *(To self)* Mankind is still in its infancy. We try, stumble, fall, fail, and try again, and we come ever closer in our toddling steps toward the open arms of our Maker...

MEMBER OF ACADEMY: Congratulations, Jacques de Vaucanson. You have done just as you said you would. Through months of labor, Employing Newton's laws of attraction by which the tides behave and the planets are known to rotate; Using calculations plotting the movement of the stars themselves across the heavens; Utilizing a system of springs and weights, gearwheels, cogs and escapements of your own construction fashioned in ratios of proven mathematical laws and proportion you have created a duck that flaps its wings, eats, and excretes...just like a duck.

(Pause. Music builds. VAUCANSON *watches duck and then—)*

VAUCANSON: Yes.

(Music building to end. VAUCANSON *watches the duck. Flap its wings, stretch its neck, and excrete. And repeat... Repeat... Repeat... Repeat... Repeat... Slightest change on* VAUCANSON's *face as he watches the duck. A slightest indication for first time in play...of doubt. Stirring music)*

END OF ACT ONE

ACT TWO

A Frog He Would A Wooing Go...

The Story of Lazarro Spallanzani's Great Labour

CHARACTERS & SETTING

HOUSEKEEPER, *old woman. Italian accent*
SPALLANZANI, *near death, or so he believes. Italian accent*
VAUCANSON, *elderly, near-senile*
CONDORCET, *middle-aged. Preferably same actor as* ABBE
   of ACT ONE

Time: 1794.

(Darkness. With candlestick and bowl, HOUSEKEEPER. Wind heard outside, whistling and banging the shutters. Distant bark of dog. Room dimly seen. Room clearly cold, dank, and draughty. Much clutter on desk. Preferably a bust of Reaumur, or portrait of Reaumur on wall. Housekeeper lights a candle with her candle. Sets down bowl of porridge. Faint croak of frogs. In candlelight, we see old man asleep with head on desk. SPALLANZANI.)

HOUSEKEEPER: *Signore...? (Pause) Signore...?*

(She has in hand a pail containing a few scraps of coal and a small shovel, having picked up these two articles by the small stove in the room. With shovel she bangs on pail. Or perhaps she bangs on the chamber pot. Great clatter either way. Lights should remain rather dim for the next few pages of play.)

SPALLANZANI: Don't wake me up, let me dream! *(Clatter continues)* Damn it, let me dream! Let me dream! The answer was there! *(Clatter continues)* Fine! Fine! All right Housekeeper, all right, enough with the banging.

(Clatter ends.)

HOUSEKEEPER: My pardons *Signore*. You are up?

SPALLANZANI: Yes.

HOUSEKEEPER: What did you dream? An answer?

SPALLANZANI: To hell with my dreams. Why don't you let in the light?

HOUSEKEEPER: The light?

SPALLANZANI: Yes, by all means, let in the light.

(HOUSEKEEPER *opens drapes. No light is let in for it is still dark.*)

HOUSEKEEPER: Look at that—completely dark. I don't see why you must awake so early.

SPALLANZANI: Experiments.

(HOUSEKEEPER *makes to exit*)

SPALLANZANI: No, don't leave me alone until we are sure we have awoken.

(*Pause.* SPALLANZANI *and* HOUSEKEEPER *in dim light. Frog croak*)

SPALLANZANI: All right, I'm up. Get out.

HOUSEKEEPER: Eat your breakfast while it is hot.

SPALLANZANI: I am eating it, I have been eating it. Now leave me alone.

(*Pause.* SPALLANZANI, *head propped in hand, closes eyes in thinking pose. Opens eyes.*)

SPALLANZANI: You linger?

HOUSEKEEPER: To be sure you do not return to sleep.

SPALLANZANI: How many times do I have to explain to you that I sometimes must think with eyes closed, but I'm not sleeping, now get out, I have much work!

HOUSEKEEPER: Yes, *Signore.*

(*She exits. He closes eyes, forehead on palm. She enters.*)

HOUSEKEEPER: *Signore?*

(*We hear gentle snoring*)

HOUSEKEEPER: *Signore?* (*She again brings shovel to pail in a frightful banging.*)

SPALLANZANI: Yes, I'm up, this time I'm up, enough with the banging. Enough with the banging! Do you want a beating?

HOUSEKEEPER: I am sorry *Signore,* I am only doing as you requested. I do not enjoy it.

(She sets down chamberpot. SPALLANZANI *has his morning vomit into the chamberpot.)*

SPALLANZANI: Fine.

HOUSEKEEPER: You are very unreasonable in the morning.

SPALLANZANI: Fine.

HOUSEKEEPER: "Do you want a beating" indeed.

SPALLANZANI: When I say I am up I am up.

HOUSEKEEPER: But perhaps you will go back to sleep—

SPALLANZANI: I couldn't sleep now if I slit my wrists, the dreams I dreamed I'll never see again...

HOUSEKEEPER: What did you dream?

SPALLANZANI: Let me ask you a question about pants. You've sewn pants before, yes?

HOUSEKEEPER: Of course.

SPALLANZANI: *(Indicating pants he wears)* Well take these pants for instance. If I were to count the number of parts—

HOUSEKEEPER: What sort of question is this?

SPALLANZANI: Just let me ask my question—

HOUSEKEEPER: It is too early for such questions.

SPALLANZANI: *(Off behind screen to pass water)* It is never too early to learn. What time is it? Where's my watch?

HOUSEKEEPER: Four-thirty o'clock.

SPALLANZANI: Four-thirty! No! Why did you let me sleep so long!

HOUSEKEEPER: Sleep is necessary. Look! See!
Completely dark.

SPALLANZANI: Dark now, but soon dawn will come,
and even before the dawn, the dawn chorus—

HOUSEKEEPER: —all the birds and their cheery songs—

SPALLANZANI: *(Derisively)* Cheery songs...all the racket
of the birds and who can concentrate with that? And
then just when it has subsided, the street cries: the fresh
fish and old chairs to mend. And kettles to mend. And
sprats alive o! And knives to grind. What is a sprat?
A kind of snail?

HOUSEKEEPER: A herring.

SPALLANZANI: *(Derisively)* Sprats alive. And buy a bird
cage, and have your boots cleaned. Buy a door mat.
Onions fine onions. Broom, broom. Spring radishes.
And just when this settles down—

HOUSEKEEPER: Not spring radishes.

SPALLANZANI: Yes, well they cry spring radishes.
I hear it. And just when this settles down—

HOUSEKEEPER: Not spring radishes. Not until spring.

SPALLANZANI: Don't interrupt. It is nearly spring.
No doubt there's an early batch to buy.

HOUSEKEEPER: This early, none worth buying.

SPALLANZANI: No of course none worth buying,
they are never worth buying—

HOUSEKEEPER: Not to you, they play havoc with your
stomach and intestines so I am not to buy them.

SPALLANZANI: Yes.

HOUSEKEEPER: They give you wind.

SPALLANZANI: No, it's not wind, how many times do I
have to explain to you that it isn't wind, it's my fragile

gizzard from years of scientific experiments. What would I care if radishes gave me a little wind, I live alone.

HOUSEKEEPER: I live with you.

SPALLANZANI: Yes you live with me. Technically. But you...what would you mind with a little wind.

HOUSEKEEPER: It is no hardship to avoid purchasing a radish if it means less wind.

SPALLANZANI: *(Erupts)* It isn't the wind I'm talking about but ulcers and great vomiting upon these floors you clean with such diligence, feed me a radish and I'll vomit my life away. *(Broods)* Why did you bring up radishes in the first place? It is always radishes. Why yet again are we talking about radishes? Where are you going, stay here. It is nearly five o'clock in the morning, do you understand, I don't want to talk about radishes, to hell with your radishes, soon the dawn chorus will begin, and then the street cries, and when that subsides, the horseclopping, the carriages on the cobbles to hell with your radishes and the rabble and all the rest of it for it won't be quiet again until it is quite dark!

(Beat)

HOUSEKEEPER: And even then, the dogs.

SPALLANZANI: *(Agreeing)* Oh yes, and the crickets.

HOUSEKEEPER: No, there are no crickets in the city.

SPALLANZANI: I hear them.

HOUSEKEEPER: Frogs, there are frogs in the city.

SPALLANZANI: The frogs are different.

HOUSEKEEPER: And frogs.

SPALLANZANI: Never you mind about the frogs.

HOUSEKEEPER: I do not like them.

SPALLANZANI: They are not here for you to like, they are here for an experiment that posterity will thank me for. Or not. To hell with posterity, I know at least its success will stick in the craw of our rival Reaumur.

HOUSEKEEPER: I do not like a hundred frogs in the house.

SPALLANZANI: I, however, *do* like a hundred frogs in the house. Now blow, and you can take the porridge with you.

HOUSEKEEPER: You have not eaten.

SPALLANZANI: I am not hungry.

HOUSEKEEPER: It stinks in here.

SPALLANZANI: Fine.

HOUSEKEEPER: How long have you been wearing those clothes?

SPALLANZANI: These clothes? I just put them on.

HOUSEKEEPER: Just last week you mean.

SPALLANZANI: Will you please get out.

HOUSEKEEPER: What are you doing with the frogs.

SPALLANZANI: You wouldn't understand.

HOUSEKEEPER: Are you dissecting them?

SPALLANZANI: No.

HOUSEKEEPER: Why not?

SPALLANZANI: Would you like me to needlessly dissect my frogs?

HOUSEKEEPER: They would then be dead.

SPALLANZANI: Then by your leave, I shall first wheel the frogs past you in a cart for you to jeer at? All the innocent little frogs?

HOUSEKEEPER: *(A joke)* Some are innocent, but most are surely sympathizers to the crown.

SPALLANZANI: You have officially been in France too long.

HOUSEKEEPER: Yes. Yes I have.

SPALLANZANI: *(Briefly sobered)* Yes...we have. You have seen the guillotine in action?

HOUSEKEEPER: Yes.

SPALLANZANI: *(Broods)* Well at least it isn't a lingering death..... It's over quickly.

HOUSEKEEPER: Not with all the speeches that are made.

SPALLANZANI: Those poor pointless souls...

HOUSEKEEPER: They say it is only the elite they do in.

SPALLANZANI: The elite? Oh stay out of it all Housekeeper. The elite! Do you know who they're in for next? Half the members of the Academy! It seems we scientists have been "consistently singled out by the royalty for special treatment." Quite right! Anyone can see looking around here that I in particular have had special treatment.

HOUSEKEEPER: You are that piece of farmland that gets the extra dung.

SPALLANZANI: Yes, that's me all right. Do you know what they've done with my friend Condorcet?

HOUSEKEEPER: Who?

SPALLANZANI: Condorcet!

HOUSEKEEPER: You have a friend?

SPALLANZANI: Yes! Though not for long. They've run him out. He's been hiding these last two months. And he! The secretary of the Academy no less! *(Broods)* No,

Housekeeper, the frogs in this experiment will not see death nor dissection...

HOUSEKEEPER: Then what sort of experiment do you have in mind that involves a hundred frogs?

SPALLANZANI: You wouldn't understand.

HOUSEKEEPER: Does it concern semen?

SPALLANZANI: Yes, as a matter of fact, it does.

HOUSEKEEPER: All your life it is semen.

SPALLANZANI: All *your* life it is semen, all everyone's lives, it is semen, it is semen. It is semen!

HOUSEKEEPER: It is no good.

SPALLANZANI: Were it not for semen, Housekeeper, it is well believed you would not exist.

HOUSEKEEPER: That is what I mean.

SPALLANZANI: Ho ho. Such sentiment. Wasn't it you going on about the birds and their pretty songs? You love our little dungball of a planet.

HOUSEKEEPER: What are you doing with the frogs and their semen?

SPALLANZANI: Nothing. I have spent a miserable week getting nowhere doing nothing on what could have been the most important series of experiments of my life. Perhaps. Perhaps not. But they are surely my last experiments.

HOUSEKEEPER: Why your last? Are you near death?

SPALLANZANI: *(Quite serious)* Yes. I am near death. *(Beat)* Oh no..Do you hear that.

HOUSEKEEPER: What.

SPALLANZANI: The peeping. It has begun.

(Dawn chorus increases in intensity.)

HOUSEKEEPER: So it has.

SPALLANZANI: The dawn is nigh and then it will be night and what have I to show for it.

HOUSEKEEPER: You have much to show for it.

SPALLANZANI: I have nothing to show for it. I have evacuated my life away.

HOUSEKEEPER: You are respected and admired in scientific circles.

SPALLANZANI: How should you know that.

HOUSEKEEPER: You told me.

SPALLANZANI: Get out. You have wasted the best part of the day. The part before the beginning.

HOUSEKEEPER: And the stove?

SPALLANZANI: Leave it.

HOUSEKEEPER: No coals?

SPALLANZANI: We are not made of coal.

HOUSEKEEPER: No we are not made of coal. But some of us are made of flint.

SPALLANZANI: What?

HOUSEKEEPER: Of flint.

SPALLANZANI: What is this?

HOUSEKEEPER: Before I take your leave, I will ask you one last time for permission to buy fabric.

SPALLANZANI: Thank God this is the last time.

HOUSEKEEPER: Your answer then still is no?

SPALLANZANI: I am not made of flint, and you are amply provided for.

HOUSEKEEPER: Flint, and I have petitioned humbly three times in as many months for—

STREET NOISES: *(From outside window:)* Fresh fish!
Old chairs to mend! Sprats alive! Sprats alive o!

SPALLANZANI: Didn't I tell you! Damn it to Hell!
Close the window!

HOUSEKEEPER: It is already closed.

SPALLANZANI: Already closed! Well then we must
seal the edges with wax—

HOUSEKEEPER: Why?

SPALLANZANI: To shut it out of course!

HOUSEKEEPER: You can't shut it out Signore.

SPALLANZANI: Can't I now.

HOUSEKEEPER: It is impossible.

SPALLANZANI: We'll see about that. A wall of cork
perhaps.

HOUSEKEEPER: It is impossible.

*(Meanwhile, from outside window, we hear various street
cries—)*

STREET NOISES: Old chairs to mend!
Kettles to mend!
Buy a bird cage!
Knives to grind!
Have your boots cleaned!
Dust o! Dust o!
Buy a door mat!
Onions fine onions!
Broom, broom!
Spring radishes!

*(At "spring radishes" SPALLANZANI points to window
triumphantly)*

HOUSEKEEPER: Ah. Spring radishes.

SPALLANZANI: You see! You see! And on the First of March.

HOUSEKEEPER: It is not the First of March. It is the Ninth of Wind.

SPALLANZANI: *(Apoplectic)* Curse you woman, radishes do not give me wind!

HOUSEKEEPER: I am talking about the new calendar.

SPALLANZANI: What new calendar. What are you saying.

HOUSEKEEPER: It is the ninth of Wind. *(Beat)* Ventose. *(Beat)* Wind.

SPALLANZANI: *(Impatient)* Yes wind. *(Then realizing—)* Oh no...don't tell me the revolutionaries have done something to the calendar!

HOUSEKEEPER: They have revolutionized it, why have you not heard about these things.

SPALLANZANI: I have better occupations. And we are not French, we are exiles.

HOUSEKEEPER: I am French. "Liberty, Equality, Fraternity."

SPALLANZANI: Shut up.

HOUSEKEEPER: Wind is the sixth month. The first month is Vintage Month, the second is Fog, the third Sleet, then Snow, then Rain, now we are in Wind.

SPALLANZANI: And there are still twelve months?

HOUSEKEEPER: Yes. Thirty days a month. But ten days a week. Every tenth day a day of rest.

SPALLANZANI: Idiots. They say they are for the people, then institute less rest.

HOUSEKEEPER: I thought you would be in favor of less rest.

SPALLANZANI: What I do I do, but I would not impose a calendar of my habits upon the people.

HOUSEKEEPER: Oh you wouldn't?

SPALLANZANI: What? What are you talking about? When was this calendar decided?

HOUSEKEEPER: In October. I mean, in Fog.

SPALLANZANI: In fog is right. Do they realize that they still cannot convince the earth from revolving around the sun in nothing less than three-hundred-and-sixty-five days and thrity days times twelve months is three-hunred-and-sixty. What will they do with five extra days?

HOUSEKEEPER: Those will be feast days. They are named Virtue, Genius—

SPALLANZANI: I don't care about any of this. Get out. The Royal Academy in havoc, my good friend Condorcet in hiding and much abused, a cantaloupe in the street turns out to be a severed head, my stomach's all atwist, leave, please...

HOUSEKEEPER: *(Finding fabric)* What is this?

SPALLANZANI: Please leave.

HOUSEKEEPER: Signore!

SPALLANZANI: What? What does it look like!

HOUSEKEEPER: A bolt of taffeta.

SPALLANZANI: It is exactly a bolt of taffeta.

HOUSEKEEPER: How long have you had this.

SPALLANZANI: I don't know—a week.

HOUSEKEEPER: And you have not told me?

SPALLANZANI: Told you what?

HOUSEKEEPER: Signore, I don't understand.

SPALLANZANI: What.

HOUSEKEEPER: But thank you, it is very fine.

SPALLANZANI: Thank you? No, no, it is not for you.

HOUSEKEEPER: This is not for me?

SPALLANZANI: No it is not for you.

HOUSEKEEPER: It's not?

SPALLANZANI: No.

HOUSEKEEPER: Who is it for then?

SPALLANZANI: Who do you think it is for?

HOUSEKEEPER: There is a woman in your life?

SPALLANZANI: Unfortunately.

HOUSEKEEPER: *(Clarifying)* Other than me there is a woman in your life?

SPALLANZANI: Please get out.

HOUSEKEEPER: I will not get out. *Signore,* I wish to register a grievance.

SPALLANZANI: Bah.

HOUSEKEEPER: I have petitioned humbly three times in as many months for fabric so that I can replace the timeworn and insupportable articles I now possess and each time you have said no no too expensive, too extravagant, no, no what do you need new dresses for—

SPALLANZANI: *(Overlapping)* What do you need new dresses for? Who are you trying to impress.

HOUSEKEEPER: There is such a thing as decency.

SPALLANZANI: There is such a thing as economy.

HOUSEKEEPER: You can nearly see through the ones I have.

SPALLANZANI: No one cares, no one cares.

HOUSEKEEPER: They are very old.

SPALLANZANI: This is all very old. Do you know how little money I possess?

HOUSEKEEPER: Yes, and to think now a whole bolt for some woman I have not even seen, it is not right—

SPALLANZANI: Oh so now you must approve all my women?

HOUSEKEEPER: Yes, all your women.

SPALLANZANI: All the countesses and concubines slinking about here—

HOUSEKEEPER: Tell me who she is.

SPALLANZANI: There is no woman.

HOUSEKEEPER: Then who is the taffeta for?

SPALLANZANI: For me of course.

HOUSEKEEPER: For you?

SPALLANZANI: For me, for me.

HOUSEKEEPER: But look at this sheen! You will look embarrassing. You are too old to parade about in—

SPALLANZANI: (Interrupting) I am not going to parade about—

HOUSEKEEPER: You will be that thing, a fop—

SPALLANZANI: Get out.

HOUSEKEEPER: They will see you and cut off your head. And you knew my situation, and you who profess to eschew all such fine things, and here.... Do not expect me to make any taffeta pants for you—

SPALLANZANI: I am worn out before dawn.

HOUSEKEEPER: I will not make pants for you to parade about after—

SPALLANZANI: Woman, the taffeta is not for me.

HOUSEKEEPER: Oh now it is not for you.

SPALLANZANI: It is for my experiments.

HOUSEKEEPER: Who is this woman.

SPALLANZANI: I am worn out before dawn!

HOUSEKEEPER: I demand an explanation!

SPALLANZANI: You demand?

HOUSEKEEPER: I don't see how you can use taffeta in an experiment.

SPALLANZANI: Oh so you don't believe me.

HOUSEKEEPER: No.

SPALLANZANI: Well I am.

HOUSEKEEPER: Then explain it then. *(Pause)* Please. *(Pause)* I would like to know.

SPALLANZANI: *(Considers, then—)* It is very involved. You wouldn't understand. It is sci-en-tific.

HOUSEKEEPER: Then I will quit your service.

SPALLANZANI: Quit my service?

HOUSEKEEPER: Yes.

SPALLANZANI: After thirty...thirty—

HOUSEKEEPER: Yes, after thirty—

SPALLANZANI: No, forty—

HOUSEKEEPER: After forty one years of service, yes. With relief.

SPALLANZANI: And where will you go?

HOUSEKEEPER: Back to Pavia.

SPALLANZANI: What, Italy? It is under siege.

HOUSEKEEPER: I will go back to Pavia with pleasure and be done with you.

SPALLANZANI: But I am near death.

HOUSEKEEPER: I am sorry that I will miss the finale.

SPALLANZANI: So go. You wouldn't understand, so why bother explaining.

HOUSEKEEPER: I have petitioned humbly three times in as many months for fabric—

SPALLANZANI: I know—

HOUSEKEEPER: —so that I can replace the timeworn and insupportable articles—

SPALLANZANI: I know—

HOUSEKEEPER: —I now possess and each time you have said—

SPALLANZANI: Yes, yes, I know what I have said.

HOUSEKEEPER: So to hell with you, goodbye. *(She is at the door, holding the full chamberpot.)*

SPALLANZANI: Leave then.

HOUSEKEEPER: I am sick of it.

SPALLANZANI: I can make my own porridge.

HOUSEKEEPER: I ask very little.

(HOUSEKEEPER exits with chamberpot. Pause. SPALLANZANI sets to work. Loud frog croak. Cuts a swath of taffeta. Begins to pin a paper pattern to the taffeta, but pricks his finger.)

SPALLANZANI: Bah! *(He impulsively crumples up paper pattern violently. Beat. Then begins to retch. Looks about for chamberpot. He cannot find it.)* You stole my chamberpot.... *(Opens door and calls out:)* You stole

my chamberpot! You stole my chamberpot! You stole
my chamberpot!

(Great amount of stomping, HOUSEKEEPER *opens door,
flings in now-empty chamberpot.* SPALLANZANI *grabs pot,
waits for it, then vomits convulsively.* HOUSEKEEPER *lingers
at door due to begrudging compassion.)*

SPALLANZANI: *(Through retches)* How did you come to
be....How did you come to be.... *(Pause)* I'm asking you
a question!

HOUSEKEEPER: Be what?

SPALLANZANI: Be what?

HOUSEKEEPER: Your Housekeeper?

SPALLANZANI: Human! I mean Human! This! You once
were not, and now you're here....

HOUSEKEEPER: Yes I am here, but soon in Pavia.

SPALLANZANI: Do you have any idea how you came
to be?

HOUSEKEEPER: You won't get me to say it.

SPALLANZANI: I'm not talking about sexual intercourse,
I am talking about the mechanism *behind* sexual
intercourse that creates life.

HOUSEKEEPER: I am leaving.

SPALLANZANI: I am trying to explain why I've been
up every night in tears for over a week, I'm trying to
explain why I purchased a bolt of fine taffeta, and you
said you will quit my service if I do not—

HOUSEKEEPER: And you must drag sex into all of it?

SPALLANZANI: No, Sex drags *us* into all of it. And here
we are. And I'll say it now—I'd rather each of us just
split in two and have done with all this...coming
together, but there's nothing to be done.

HOUSEKEEPER: But as the church says, "there is pleasure too, at coming together, which God in his mercy arranged for."

SPALLANZANI: Pleasure? To hell with pleasure! It only distracts us from what truly matters. How much better if God had made the act excruciating, so that each couple would have to pause in the middle of sex if only to ask, "why again are we doing this?" Why indeed! That is how it would be if I were God.

HOUSEKEEPER: You would be an unpopular God.

SPALLANZANI: So be it.

HOUSEKEEPER: I would not worship you.

SPALLANZANI: And why not?! When have you ever been with a man?

HOUSEKEEPER: If you do not explain to me what a bolt of taffeta has to do with this, I swear to you I will return to Pavia within the hour.

SPALLANZANI: *(Derisively)* Within the hour.

HOUSEKEEPER: *(Earnest to point of tears)* I mean it. I mean it. I mean it.

(Pause)

SPALLANZANI: Come here... *(Pause)* Come here!
(He holds up a vial.) This is a liquid, like water is a liquid, like wine is a liquid, like milk is a liquid. But this liquid, in the womb of a woman, creates life.

HOUSEKEEPER: Semen.

SPALLANZANI: Yes, And I want to discover exactly what it is in semen that initiates life, and where it is—in the watery part, or in the denser part containing the worms.

HOUSEKEEPER: Worms?

SPALLANZANI: *(With vial)* Believe it or not, there are thousands of spermatick worms swimming about in here...Some even think these worms are essential to reproduction.

HOUSEKEEPER: But you don't?

SPALLANZANI: I don't Housekeeper, no. Parasites are found everywhere, in our blood, our intestines—these spermatick worms are merely parasites that have taken up home in my testes. It doesn't make sense that I would come from a worm.

HOUSEKEEPER: I think it makes much sense.

SPALLANZANI: Thank you. But look—so many sperm are found in semen that it would mean an incredible waste of potential life, and it is not conceivable that a God would allow such waste.

HOUSEKEEPER: I think I've never heard anything more conceivable.

SPALLANZANI: You are very cynical, Housekeeper.

HOUSEKEEPER: And you, what are you?

SPALLANZANI: Don't change the subject. I'm working with frogs because I like frogs, and god knows they're easier to work with than humans. Not to mention that with *frogs* I can use artificial insemination. I can paint the semen onto the eggs directly! No one has thought of that before!

HOUSEKEEPER: Not even Reaumur?

SPALLANZANI: *(Twisting face)* Reaumur? Reaumur's greatest scientific achievement will be when he discovers his own bottom...and then shoves two fingers up it!

HOUSEKEEPER: And then he will publish his findings.

SPALLANZANI: *(Amused with her joke)* Hear thatReaumur?

HOUSEKEEPER: *(Again impatient)* But what does this have to do with a bolt of taffeta.

SPALLANZANI: I'm telling you!

HOUSEKEEPER: You're not telling me!

SPALLANZANI: It comes down to this. There is no point in experimenting with frogs if I can't afterward apply what I've learned to humans. Right?

HOUSEKEEPER: But frogs are not humans.

SPALLANZANI: The difference is trivial!

HOUSEKEEPER: You think frogs and humans are the same!? I can't understand—

SPALLANZANI: No, you can, you can, stop pretending you're thick and just try...There are those who believe that unlike a human, a frog does not need semen to fertilize its egg. So If I'm going to work with frogs— and damn it, I want to work with frogs—I first have to prove, once and for all, that semen is required, that the frogs *can't go it alone*...that they, in that, are like human beings.... Now...how do I do that?

HOUSEKEEPER: How.

SPALLANZANI: Well this very issue came up at a party I went to—

HOUSEKEEPER: You?

SPALLANZANI: Yes. Don't interrupt. I was at a party—

HOUSEKEEPER: Where?

SPALLANZANI: It was a ball at a chateau.

HOUSEKEEPER: Really?

SPALLANZANI: Yes, there's no reason to be so surprised. I was at a party—

HOUSEKEEPER: When was this?

SPALLANZANI: Not long ago.

HOUSEKEEPER: How long?

SPALLANZANI: It was...fifty years ago...I was new to Paris, I barely knew the language, but yes, damn it, I was at a party.

HOUSEKEEPER: Fine.

SPALLANZANI: Fine! And I met a fellow scientist by the duck pond, and the frogs were quite loud and it was in casting back to events of that night... *(Counts)* A scientist, an emission from his privates, and his subsequently damp clothing...that I had a revelation.

HOUSEKEEPER: I am ready.

SPALLANZANI: *(Containing excitement)* All right... Housekeeper...can you think of a situation in which a man and a woman has sexual intercourse...stay here, stay here...the man remains in the woman until he ejaculates...and yet they both can be utterly assured there will be no pregnancy?

(Pause)

HOUSEKEEPER: *(Clearly uncomfortable)* When a man uses.... When the man's...semen...is contained.

SPALLANZANI: *(Nearly embracing her, near tears)* Yes! Exactly! Exactly! And therefore none of the frog eggs should develop if the frogs mate while each male frog is wearing...a pair of tight-fitting taffeta pants! And that is why I am determined to make tweny-nine pairs of tight-fitting taffeta pants as soon as possible, and that is why I have been up these miserable sleepless nights, being occupied in the unforseeably difficult task of constructing twenty-nine very small pairs of tight-fitting taffeta pants, for frogs.

(Pause)

HOUSEKEEPER: Ah. *(Pause. She turns to leave.)*

SPALLANZANI: Where are you going?

HOUSEKEEPER: Pavia!

SPALLANZANI: Good God, haven't I just done what you asked?!

HOUSEKEEPER: *(With fury)* So I am to come in every morning and be...and be mocked by these frogs fashionably dressed—

SPALLANZANI: This isn't about fashion, it's about Life, Life—

HOUSEKEEPER: It's about loyal service.

SPALLANZANI: Holy Christ you have not heard a word I've said—

HOUSEKEEPER: They will be wearing fabric meant for me—

SPALLANZANI: *(Shrill)* It was never meant for you! It was never meant for you!

HOUSEKEEPER: This...is meant for you. *(She spits, exits, slamming the door.)*

SPALLANZANI: Just tell me, what's the trick for pinning taffeta together? Why is it so damned slippery!

(The door is opened by the HOUSEKEEPER *and slammed again.* SPALLANZANI *sets to work on pants. Sound of carriages on cobbles outside window. Frog croak. Exhalations and great curses of frustration. His hands are clearly trembling due to age.)*

SPALLANZANI: Damn these hands!

(Outside the window:)

STREET NOISES: Knives to grind!
Buy a bird cage!
Knives to grind!
Have your boots cleaned!

Dust o! Dust o!
Buy a door mat!
Onions fine onions!
Sprats alive!
Sprats alive o!

SPALLANZANI: *(Derisively)* Sprats...

(Thunderstorm. A miserable example of pants is completed. Holds it up for inspection. Pulls each end of waist to test durability. It splits down the middle. Lights begin to fade. Takes match to candle. He listens to church bells ring.)

SPALLANZANI: And there's the day. Done. Damn it to Hell.

(He shoves several of his materials off desk. Housekeeper enters.)

SPALLANZANI: Why haven't you left yet.

HOUSEKEEPER: I have found a coach that will take me as far as Milan for a reasonable price. It leaves tomorrow morning.

SPALLANZANI: I have no traveling money for you.

HOUSEKEEPER: And I would be a fool to expect any. There is a woman here who wants to see you.

SPALLANZANI: Where?

HOUSEKEEPER: At the front door.

SPALLANZANI: Why didn't you say so? Who is she?

(HOUSEKEEPER shrugs.)

SPALLANZANI: What does she want?

HOUSEKEEPER: To see you.

SPALLANZANI: About what?

HOUSEKEEPER: *(Shrugs)* She seems upset.

SPALLANZANI: Well I'm working.

HOUSEKEEPER: What should I tell her?

SPALLANZANI: That I'm busy.

HOUSEKEEPER: I will tell her you are busy with your pants and can't see anyone for a few days.

SPALLANZANI: Don't tell her that.

HOUSEKEEPER: I will tell her that.

SPALLANZANI: Fine. Fine! Send her in.

(Pause. CONDORCET, *secretary of the Royal Academy rushes in, shuts door behind him, pale, panicked, wild-eyed, drenched, and wearing women's clothing. Gown, wig, makeup ill-applied. He is missing a shoe, his articles are in disarray. Heavy French accent.)*

CONDORCET: Lazarro, thank God!

SPALLANZANI: What is this?

CONDORCET: Please, You must hide me! Immediately!

SPALLANZANI: Jean? Is that you?

CONDORCET: Yes, it is I, Jean Condorcet. Your friend.

SPALLANZANI: I thought you were in hiding.

CONDORCET: My hiding place has been discovered. Someone leaked. No matter. Praise be to God I made it here. I am nearly collapsed with exhaustion.

SPALLANZANI: *(Calling out from door)* Housekeeper, damn it, this is a man, a great man, and you knew it! Now get some water! Quickly! *(To* CONDORCET*)* A disguise, that was smart thinking.

CONDORCET: It was the work of panicked minutes, it is a most ill-fit.

SPALLANZANI: No, it is convincing.

CONDORCET: *(Gravely worried)* It is not *too* attractive,
I trust. I do not wish to call any attention to myself if
I am to escape the city.

SPALLANZANI: No, be assured, you are not too attractive.

CONDORCET: In the downpour, through Paris, first here
then there, always one step ahead of the *gendarmes*,
seeking asylum with old friends, but all my old
friends—half have been arrested already, and the
other half cast me back out on the street. *(Angry at shoes)*
These shoes make things impossible.

SPALLANZANI: But the *gendarmes*—they will not follow
you here, will they?

CONDORCET: Yes, they might! That is why you must
hide me, or they will arrest you too for harboring me.

SPALLANZANI: Arrest me? But I am Italian!

CONDORCET: Please, I fear for my life—

SPALLANZANI: But I have no place to hide you.

CONDORCET: Anywhere! I just need a few days.
Don't you have a cellar?

SPALLANZANI: This is the cellar! I am very poor.
But look, is it wise to even stay in the city?

CONDORCET: It's true, my only hope is to flee Paris,
for if I am caught it is surely the guillotine which I
will never allow, which is why I have this....

SPALLANZANI: What is it?

CONDORCET: Arsenic.

SPALLANZANI: *(Looking into eyes)* No man...no....

CONDORCET: I won't suffer execution.... *(Pulling out of
bosom a large bundle of papers tied with string)* but look,
I'll leave Paris, but first a day of rest, and time to pass

on this manuscript to some former member of the Academy sympathetic to the cause.

SPALLANZANI: What do you mean, "former member"?

CONDORCET: The National Convention has disbanded the Royal Academy of Sciences.

SPALLANZANI: They can't!

CONDORCET: Hah, can't they now. They have. "An elitist institution" they called it and snip snap. But we will go on, we must.

SPALLANZANI: What is the manuscript?

CONDORCET: Oh Lazarro, it is the culmination of my life's work! I completed it while in hiding. I was to hand the work off to a man tonight in fact, but I was flushed out before I could meet him.

SPALLANZANI: The topic, is it mathematics?

CONDORCET: No, it is a Sketch for a Historical Picture of the Progress of the Human Mind!

SPALLANZANI: *(Agape)* You say there is progress?

CONDORCET: *(Solemnly)* I know there is, Lazarro, I know there is. And you do too. In the tenth epoch, there will be equality among the classes and people will improve physically, intellectually, morally... *(Reads from work solemnly, much dignity in his muddied gown:)* "I picture posterity and how welcome is this picture of the human race, freed from all its chains—

SPALLANZANI: *(Hearing a distant knock)* Ssh.

CONDORCET: —released from the domination of chance, advancing with a firm and sure step in the path of truth, virtue—

SPALLANZANI: Ssh!

(Distant knock on front door)

CONDORCET: Did you hear that?

SPALLANZANI: Yes!

CONDORCET: It was a knock on the door!

SPALLANZANI: The gendarmes!

CONDORCET: Lazarro, what can I do?!

SPALLANZANI: Get out.

CONDORCET: I'll hide behind the drapes.

SPALLANZANI: No they'll see you.

CONDORCET: Then what can I do?

SPALLANZANI: You can get out. Try the window.

CONDORCET: It's too small. What about under your desk!

SPALLANZANI: No no, there are frogs underneath, they will be crushed—

(Pause. CONDORCET *looks at the vial of poison in his hand.* SPALLANZANI *wrestles with* CONDORCET *for the vial.)*

SPALLANZANI: No...no... Put it away!

(A knock on the door. HOUSEKEEPER *enters.)*

HOUSEKEEPER: There is a man here who wants to see you.

SPALLANZANI: Just one?

HOUSEKEEPER: Yes.

SPALLANZANI: Did he say who he is?

HOUSEKEEPER: *(Shrugs)* He is old.

SPALLANZANI: What does he want?

HOUSEKEEPER: To see you.

SPALLANZANI: About what?

HOUSEKEEPER: I couldn't care less.

SPALLANZANI: Housekeeper! Is he armed?

HOUSEKEEPER: I will send him in.

(She exits)

SPALLANZANI: No, wait!

(An elderly man enters. Quite frail, appalling condition. Coughing wretchedly. It is JACQUES DE VAUCANSON. *Pronounced French accent. Approaching a senile parody of his* ACT ONE *self.)*

VAUCANSON: Monsieur Spallanzani?

SPALLANZANI: Yes.

VAUCANSON: My pardons for disturbing you at such a late hour. I—Oh! And you have company...

*(*VAUCANSON *winks and nudges knowingly for he has noticed a female form hiding not very well.)*

CONDORCET: Jacques?

VAUCANSON: *(Flirting)* Do I know you?

CONDORCET: It is I!

VAUCANSON: Madam?

CONDORCET: No!

VAUCANSON: *(Amazement)* Jean?

SPALLANZANI: *(To* CONDORCET*)* Is he one of us?

VAUCANSON: I have been all over Paris in search of you.

CONDORCET: *(To* SPALLANZANI*)* This is Jacques de Vaucanson, he is the man I was to give my manuscript to tonight.

VAUCANSON: *(To* CONDORCET*)* Yes, but I heard you had to flee.

SPALLANZANI: *(Calling out from door)* Housekeeper!
A drink for this man! Monsieur Vaucanson, it is an
honor to meet such an eminent scientist.

VAUCANSON: The honor is mine.

SPALLANZANI: I am no scientist, but... *(Now truly
noticing)* ...but how old you are! I beg your pardon
but was there no one better suited for such a grueling
assignment?

VAUCANSON: *(Making an unwitting mockery of* ACT
ONE*)* I'm worn out, it's true. But we must push on.
If we do not strive, then what can posterity hope for?!

SPALLANZANI: But how did you know to come here?

VAUCANSON: I received a tip from one of the *gendarmes*
who knew Jean was headed in this general direction.

SPALLANZANI: *(Panicked)* They knew?! Then they will
wind up here, surely!

VAUCANSON: *(To* CONDORCET*)* A disguise, that was
smart thinking.

CONDORCET: It was the work of panicked minutes,
and the rain made a shambles of it.

VAUCANSON: No, it looks fine.

CONDORCET: It is not too attractive, I hope.

SPALLANZANI: It's not.

VAUCANSON: I am not so sure.

SPALLANZANI: You need to get out.

CONDORCET: For an attractive lady alone on the
outskirts of the city might arouse suspicion. Ideally,
I should appear past my prime.

VAUCANSON: Perhaps even a washerwoman.

CONDORCET: You must help me!

(HOUSEKEEPER *enters with water*)

VAUCANSON: You can't be too careful. Perhaps you should swap clothing with his Housekeeper, her clothes seem more down-at-the-heels.

HOUSEKEEPER: *(Indignant)* Don't I know it.

CONDORCET: *(To* VAUCANSON*)* Yes, perhaps you are right. We will change immediately.

HOUSEKEEPER: Change?

SPALLANZANI: Yes, exchange dresses with the man.

HOUSEKEEPER: But I am not of a mind.

VAUCANSON: Give him your smock, quickly!

SPALLANZANI: Damn it woman, this is a great man! His life is on the line!

HOUSEKEEPER: *Signore,* you wish to take the very dress from my body. I am sorry but no, I cannot allow it. I am after all in your service no longer.

CONDORCET: *(Desperate, near tears)* Please! Please!

HOUSEKEEPER: No. Jean-Marie Condorcet. Mathematician, philosopher, supporter of the Revolution and member of the revolutionary Legislative Assembly and Convention. Fleeing the city dressed as a woman, you will be discovered in a country inn outside of Paris and arrested. Two months later, at the age of fifty-one, you will be found dead in your cell, officially from exhaustion, though more likely from your little vial of poison.

(HOUSEKEEPER *exits. Pause*)

SPALLANZANI: *(Having heard only the* HOUSEKEEPER's *"No".)* Well, so be it.

VAUCANSON: You look fine without the smock.

SPALLANZANI: This is the manuscript.

VAUCANSON: *(Reading)* "Man will not always be corrupted by greed, fear and envy. He will one day be restored to the rights and dignity of his nature!"

CONDORCET: *(Overlapping, reciting from memory)* "He will one day be restored to the rights and dignity of his nature!"

SPALLANZANI: You can't stay here.

CONDORCET: But friend, you are my last hope.

SPALLANZANI: But of course I'm not. At the very least, take a room in a country inn, you will surely be safer there than here. Go now, quickly, before they gain anymore ground.

CONDORCET: But—

SPALLANZANI: No, this is for the best, I'm thinking of you.

CONDORCET: If we but had your Housekeeper's smock—

SPALLANZANI: Forget the smock—

CONDORCET: But—

SPALLANZANI: Hang the smock! Here, drink this. Now you must go.

CONDORCET: Thank you. I should like to have stayed, I am very tired. *(Pause)* But perhaps you are right.

SPALLANZANI: Good then. Farewell.

CONDORCET: I'm off.

VAUCANSON: Safe passage.

CONDORCET: Farewell.

SPALLANZANI: Godspeed.

CONDORCET: Thank you.

VAUCANSON: Good luck my friend.

CONDORCET: We'll meet again.

SPALLANZANI: Of course.

CONDORCET: Farewell!

VAUCANSON: *Au revoir.*

(Beat)

CONDORCET: I'm off.

SPALLANZANI: *Au revoir.*

VAUCANSON: *Au revoir.*

(CONDORCET *reluctantly exits. And as* VAUCANSON *is about to exit:)*

SPALLANZANI: And you, Jacques de Vaucanson.

VAUCANSON: We have met before.

SPALLANZANI: Your clockwork duck will survive you.

VAUCANSON: Its parts were more durable than my own.

SPALLANZANI: It will be exhibited by Bontems, the famous maker of the mechanical singing birds. The duck will end up in the cabinet of curiosities of a certain Mister Gassner of Karkov in the Ukraine. This cabinet, and the duck with it, will burn to ashes in 1879, the same year Albert Einstein was born, Cetewayo, king of the Zulus, was deposed, and Robert Louis Stevenson wrote Travels with a Donkey.

VAUCANSON: And you, Lazarro Spallanzani, will die of a urinary-tract infection in Pavia. Your corpse will fall into the hands of your rival, Reaumur, who will remove your penis and testicles out of maliciousness and put them on display in a jar at the university museum, where they will stay for over two-hundred years.

SPALLANZANI: That is most upsetting. God damn Reaumur.

VAUCANSON: Reaumur's corpse will be seized after his death by your colleagues, who will decapitate him and place his head in a jar, and for over two-hundred years his head will sit on a shelf next to your testicles.

SPALLANZANI: The result of our struggles is meaningless.

VAUCANSON: Yet the struggles themselves are noble—

SPALLANZANI: Life is a difficult movement of the bowels. If we persevere, it is because we haven't a choice. Call that noble.

VAUCANSON: And yet...

SPALLANZANI: *(Conceding)* And yet...

VAUCANSON: *(Decisively)* And yet.

SPALLANZANI: Yes. Yes... Now get out. Out. Out.

(SPALLANZANI kicks VAUCANSON to the door, hurls him out door and he slams it shut. Gathers materials still on floor. Places them back on desk. Sits down. Shoves materials off of desk. Knock on door. HOUSEKEEPER enters with bowl.)

HOUSEKEEPER: They are all gone?

SPALLANZANI: We still might get a call from soldiers come to arrest me....

HOUSEKEEPER: I will tell them you are busy with your pants.

SPALLANZANI: That man's dress was far nicer than yours. Why didn't you swap when you had the chance?

HOUSEKEEPER: It was not a dress for housekeeping.

SPALLANZANI: I thought you were done with housekeeping.

HOUSEKEEPER: I am done housekeeping for you, but the dress still is no good. I am not returning to Pavia for the balls and banquets, am I...

SPALLANZANI: You are returning to glimpse once more the Ticino River from the old town where you sat with your lover when you were young and comely.

HOUSEKEEPER: I couldn't give a curse for the foul Ticino.

SPALLANZANI: Perhaps you've never glimpsed it with a lover. *(Pause)* Perhaps you never had a lover.

HOUSEKEEPER: Eat.

SPALLANZANI: Ah, porridge. I shall miss your cooking.

(HOUSEKEEPER *meanwhile picking up the materials lying on the floor, stifles a snicker.)*

SPALLANZANI: What was that?

HOUSEKEEPER: My pardons, *Signore.* A sneeze.

SPALLANZANI: A sneeze indeed. What is it? You did something to the porridge? As a last gesture you have spit in it.

HOUSEKEEPER: No. It is nothing.

SPALLANZANI: *(Seeing her with materials in hand)* Or is it my patterns?

HOUSEKEEPER: No.

SPALLANZANI: Yes it is. I know that little smugness of yours.

HOUSEKEEPER: Have any of your frogs been fitted out yet in your pants?

SPALLANZANI: I have to make them first don't I.

HOUSEKEEPER: *(Pointing to pattern)* How will you get their feet through so small a space at the bottom of the leg?

SPALLANZANI: Eh?

HOUSEKEEPER: Frogs have large feet.

SPALLANZANI: I know they have large feet.

HOUSEKEEPER: I suppose you'll just push.

SPALLANZANI: Yes, I'll just push, it won't be difficult. *(Pause)* The pants must be tight!

HOUSEKEEPER: Good luck then.

SPALLANZANI: They must be tight!

HOUSEKEEPER: Fine.

SPALLANZANI: There can be no leakage! *(Broods)* But I see your point. But I cannot contrive another way. A hook and eye perhaps?

(HOUSEKEEPER *stifles another snicker)*

SPALLANZANI: *(Fed up, pushes bowl off desk)* I am not hungry. Take this. Get out.

(She picks up bowl and makes to leave)

SPALLANZANI: I suppose you have a better way?

HOUSEKEEPER: No.

SPALLANZANI: You do.

HOUSEKEEPER: I can't think of anything.

SPALLANZANI: Well then stay out of it.

HOUSEKEEPER: A drawstring perhaps. *(She exits.)*

SPALLANZANI: A drawstring? Come back here! A drawstring you say?

HOUSEKEEPER: At the bottom of each leg. The pants legs can be quite baggy, but then pulled in at the ankle and kept there with a knot.

SPALLANZANI: But the string will fall off.

HOUSEKEEPER: Do you know nothing? You would keep it there by sewing it into a hem of course.

SPALLANZANI: *(Feigning helplessness)* A hem...

(Pause. Blank face of SPALLANZANI. *She hastily grabs fabric on desk and demonstrates—)*

HOUSEKEEPER: You see, and you turn it over, with the string, then sew it shut, but leave an opening for the string to dangle out.

(She makes to exit again.)

SPALLANZANI: What sort of string? Thread would work, yes? I have strong thread.

HOUSEKEEPER: It stinks in here. *(She begins to exit.)*

SPALLANZANI: I am not using all the taffeta... I won't be needing the entire bolt.

HOUSEKEEPER: Oh with the way you sew you will...

SPALLANZANI: There is a chance.

HOUSEKEEPER: What do I care?

SPALLANZANI: Help me, and you can have what is left.

HOUSEKEEPER: I will be in Pavia long before you are finished.

SPALLANZANI: If you assisted me, the pants could be completed sooner and you would have all that remained to take with you.

HOUSEKEEPER: Why are you in such a rush?

SPALLANZANI: I am near death.

HOUSEKEEPER: It stinks in here.

SPALLANZANI: Stop saying that. Will you or will you not? There's a good seven hours before dawn, twenty-nine pairs of pants divided by two, fourteen and a half, by seven hours, a little more than two pairs an hour per person.

HOUSEKEEPER: It can't be done.

SPALLANZANI: It can!

HOUSEKEEPER: Why should I help you?

SPALLANZANI: I told you. For the taffeta.

HOUSEKEEPER: Do you think my life is ruled by fabric?

SPALLANZANI: *(Agape)* Isn't it?

HOUSEKEEPER: *(With bit of relish)* But you need my help.

SPALLANZANI: Yes I need your help. And...more than that....

HOUSEKEEPER: I'm listening.

SPALLANZANI: Well I don't think you'll credit it but... it's true—

HOUSEKEEPER: Tell me...

SPALLANZANI: Well...damn it...after forty-one years... you owe me.

HOUSEKEEPER: I owe you?!

SPALLANZANI: Well find your own reason then!

HOUSEKEEPER: I don't know why you bother at all!

SPALLANZANI: What do you mean? With what?

HOUSEKEEPER: This! Your work—

SPALLANZANI: *(Exasperated)* Why? I told you why.

HOUSEKEEPER: Did you?

SPALLANZANI: Why does anyone do anything?!

HOUSEKEEPER: *(Sincere)* Why *does* anyone do anything?

(Long pause)

SPALLANZANI: *(Feebly)* ...Why...

HOUSEKEEPER: Why have I persisted in cleaning your chamberpot every day for all these years.

SPALLANZANI: You have a nurturing personality. You could not live alone. You would shrivel.

HOUSEKEEPER: You would shrivel.

SPALLANZANI: Are you going to help me with my pants or not?

(Pause. And the HOUSEKEEPER *at last relents and crosses to the table.)*

SPALLANZANI: There we are!

(Pleased, SPALLANZANI *shows her a seat.* HOUSEKEEPER *picks up needle and thread)*

HOUSEKEEPER: And all for semen.

SPALLANZANI: As soon as I acquired my first microscope sixty years ago, it was the first thing I examined, and it shall be my last...

HOUSEKEEPER: What did you do?

SPALLANZANI: What do you mean.

HOUSEKEEPER: When you first acquired your microscope. Where did you obtain the semen? Did you have frogs even then?

SPALLANZANI: You have so little imagination that you cannot construe where and how I might have obtained some semen?

HOUSEKEEPER: It's not sold in shops.

SPALLANZANI: Are you baiting me?

HOUSEKEEPER: I am sincere.

SPALLANZANI: I will tell you plainly then that I manipulated my own privatees in a fashion thereby obtaining a sample.

HOUSEKEEPER: *(Shocked and intrigued)* Did you? What do you mean, "in a fashion"?

SPALLANZANI: Forget it.

HOUSEKEEPER: Does this have something to do with masturbation?

SPALLANZANI: *(Impatiently)* Yes, it has everything to do with it.

HOUSEKEEPER: *(Still more shocked and intrigued)* Really? And where did you commit this sin?

SPALLANZANI: Sin indeed.

HOUSEKEEPER: In Pavia?

SPALLANZANI: Yes in Pavia.

HOUSEKEEPER: Have you masturbated here in Paris?

SPALLANZANI: Enough of this.

HOUSEKEEPER: Have you masturbated in this room?

SPALLANZANI: I said enough.

HOUSEKEEPER: *(Suddenly aware of the chair she is in)* Do you sit down when you do it?

SPALLANZANI: Good God woman, have you never done it?!

(HOUSEKEEPER, *without a word, puts down sewing materials and makes to exit*)

SPALLANZANI: Where are you going?

HOUSEKEEPER: I am leaving.

SPALLANZANI: Are you making tea?

HOUSEKEEPER: No.

SPALLANZANI: You're coming back aren't you? *(Realizing)* You're not pretending to have modesty!

HOUSEKEEPER: I do have modesty.

SPALLANZANI: Housekeeper, tell me truthfully, you've never had a lover, have you?

HOUSEKEEPER: *(Lashing back)* You, the Great Fornicator, do what you will, but I have my beliefs—

SPALLANZANI: Who are you calling the Great Fornicator?

HOUSEKEEPER: You are the Great Fornicator.

SPALLANZANI: Oh I see!

HOUSEKEEPER: Intercourse before marriage is wrong—

SPALLANZANI: Yes—

HOUSEKEEPER: —and afterso its purpose is for making children! I am not ashamed of my virginity!

SPALLANZANI: But I've said the same thing all along!

(Pause. HOUSEKEEPER intrigued.)

HOUSEKEEPER: And yet you've never married....

(Silence from SPALLANZANI)

HOUSEKEEPER: You *Signore* have never been with a woman?

SPALLANZANI: No I have not.

HOUSEKEEPER: Not one?

SPALLANZANI: No.

HOUSEKEEPER: In all your life?

SPALLANZANI: Let's just drop it.

HOUSEKEEPER: So all these years—

SPALLANZANI: Yes.

HOUSEKEEPER: *(A statement)* So.

(A brief moment between them)

SPALLANZANI: Yes. *(Beat)* Yes.

HOUSEKEEPER: Why? Why no lover?

SPALLANZANI: I was busy.... Or because no one would have me...or no, I refused and I refuse to have sex for mere pleasure's sake, and I refuse to procreate if I don't know why I even exist....

HOUSEKEEPER: Were you never attracted to a woman?

SPALLANZANI: If I copulated out of blind attraction, if I didn't think about what it all meant I'd be no different and no better than Johann Carl Wilcke over there.

HOUSEKEEPER: Over where?

SPALLANZANI: There. That one.

HOUSEKEEPER: *(Touched, actually)* You have named your frogs.

SPALLANZANI: Yes, after great men of our age.

HOUSEKEEPER: Who is Wilcke?

SPALLANZANI: He discovered the concept of specific heat—the amount of heat required to raise the temperature of a unit mass one degree.

HOUSEKEEPER: *(Intrigued, pointing to another frog)* And who is that?

SPALLANZANI: That one with the spots is Antoine Lavoisier. Among other accomplishments, he revolutionized the language of chemistry.

HOUSEKEEPER: And that croaking one there?

SPALLANZANI: William Herschel. His was the largest reflecting telescope ever built and with it he discovered Uranus, the first planet to be revealed in over two thousand years. And this hopping bastard here is Francis Glisson, who explained how the gall bladder discharges bile only when it is needed. And there, Andreas Marggraaf, and there, Anders Celsius and Johannes Kepler and Joseph Black and Henry Cavendish and Allesandro Volta and Jan Ingen-Housz and Claude Bertholllet. Each one has a story and we will make pants for them all!

HOUSEKEEPER: And Lazarro Spallanzani. You too deserve pants. For your work in casting doubt on the theory of spontaneous generation, and for your development of artificial insemination, you will be known as one of the great experimentalists of the eighteenth century. But due to variables you could not have foreseen, you will still conclude wrongly that spermatick worms are only worms and have no part in reproduction. You will never know that you got it wrong. You will not survive to see the year 1875, when Wilhelm Hertwig will be the first to observe the fecundation of an egg by sperm—that we are fertilized by what you call worms, just as other so-called worms turn us in our graves to dust. *(Finishing a pair of pants)* There. That is one.

SPALLANZANI: Fine. Shall we have a fitting? Who shall it be?

HOUSEKEEPER: Who is this one?

SPALLANZANI: That is Francis Hauksbee, producer of a useful electrostatic generator.

HOUSEKEEPER: Are there any women?

SPALLANZANI: Have you not heard a word I've said? We are putting pants on *male* frogs—

HOUSEKEEPER: But you could still name one after a woman.

SPALLANZANI: No. That's too confusing. And no women scientists come to mind—

HOUSEKEEPER: You mentioned once a...Chamanet.

SPALLANZANI: Chatelet? Gabrielle du Chatelet?

HOUSEKEEPER: Yes, what about her?

SPALLANZANI: No. We're using Hauksbee. Get back to work.

(A pronounced sigh of resignation from HOUSEKEEPER.)

SPALLANZANI: I said no.

HOUSEKEEPER: Fine.

SPALLANZANI: All right, look, all the twenty-nine female frogs, every one can be named Gabrielle du Chatelet. If I remember correctly, she died in childbirth. Now if our trousers fail, she'll give birth to three thousand progeny.

HOUSEKEEPER: That's fine.

SPALLANZANI: *(Having fitted pants)* Well, there's one fitted frog.

HOUSEKEEPER: So you will stay in Paris til you die?

SPALLANZANI: It is not a long wait.

HOUSEKEEPER: You should return to Pavia.

SPALLANZANI: With you? That's a horrible idea.

HOUSEKEEPER: There's no reason to stay.

SPALLANZANI: Sssh! Listen...

(Cricket chirp)

SPALLANZANI: And you said there were no crickets in the city!

(Cricket chirp and frog croak up to unnaturally high levels as lights dim. We hear birdsong. SPALLANZANI *awakes.)*

SPALLANZANI: Birds? ...Those are birds...robins I think.... *(Realizing)* Oh christ, I fell asleep! Housekeeper?....Housekeeper?!

(We hear only a gentle, or actually rather pronounced, snoring from Housekeeper, who is asleep in chair)

SPALLANZANI: It will soon be dawn and what have I to show for it? Yes, go on, snooze on, then abandon me....

(He then notices a collection of small pants near her. He holds up pants and counts them as lights slowly rise. Birdsong heard.)

SPALLANZANI: One, two, three...eight, ten...one two three four...twenty...twenty-six, twenty-seven, twenty-eight, plus one on Hauksbee...twenty-nine...she did it, the old cow, twenty-nine pairs of tight-fitting taffeta pants....

(He finds an old blanket and gently drapes it over sleeping HOUSEKEEPER. Tucks it to chin. Kisses her)

SPALLANZANI: ...dark now...dark now...but soon dawn will come, and even now, the dawn chorus...and then the street cries...the fresh fish and old chairs to mend. *(Pause)* And kettles to mend. And sprats alive O!....sprats alive.... *(Derisively)* Sprats.... *(Shrugging)* Well...there is that at least....they are alive... *(Relishing)* Sprats....alive...O!.... *(A trial run)* ...Spallanzani alive O... *(Shouting)* Spallanzani alive O!

(His shout however is cut short by a truly violent coughing fit. HOUSEKEEPER stirs in sleep. And he, resigned, exhausted, awed:)

SPALLANZANI:....Well let it. Let it begin then. Let it. Let the day become...beguile...bewilder...benumb...bedim... and then...beget...then beget....yet....another....

(Music louder, and in growing light, CHATELET revealed)

CHATELET: *(Sung)* Awake my Paris...
Stir from thy slumberings
The worlds you now strive in
Shall be snuffed and forgotten
Come the dawn....
Bid farewell and return

To this one Dream we share....
Paris... Awake... Awake... Awake... Awake...

(Stirring music continues through curtain call.)

END OF PLAY